THRESHOLD
BIBLE STUDY

The CREED of the CHURCH

STEPHEN J. BINZ

TWENTY-THIRD
PUBLICATIONS
twentythirdpublications.com

Second Printing 2025

TWENTY-THIRD PUBLICATIONS
977 Hartford Turnpike Unit A
Waterford, CT 06385
(860) 437-3012 or (800) 321-0411
twentythirdpublications.com

Image credit: page xii, parishioners - _KUBE_stock.adobe.com

ISBN: 978-1-62785-826-7
Printed in the U.S.A.

Contents

LESSONS 13–18

LESSONS 19–24

LESSONS 25–30

What People Are Saying about *Threshold Bible Study*

"The books in Stephen Binz's *Threshold Bible Study* read like *lectio divina* meditations from the monastic tradition, but with fascinating historical insights about the biblical characters and authors. He has a gift for making these ancient texts speak an urgent but compelling word to us today, inviting us to read ourselves into the great drama of salvation history. He nourishes the roots of our Christian faith in the rich soil of Judaism, and he presents the Bible as a single fountain with an endlessly fresh supply of water for anyone thirsting for the Lord."

Thomas Esposito, O. Cist., *Professor of Theology, University of Dallas*

"*Threshold Bible Study* offers profound and valuable insights into Scripture. It helps us discover the meaning of the word of God in today's context. Stephen Binz has truly engaged himself in a prophetic and relevant mission."

Julie George S.Sp.S., *Women's rights lawyer with Streevani–The Voice of Women, India*

"The Church has called Scripture a 'font' and 'wellspring' for the spiritual life. *Threshold Bible Study* is one of the best sources for tapping into the biblical font. *Threshold Bible Study* offers you an encounter with the Word that will make your heart come alive."

Dr. Tim Gray, *President of the Augustine Institute*

"In the volumes of his *Threshold Bible Study*, Stephen Binz gives us a rich treasury for nurturing our faith with the power of the biblical word. Besides his fine Bible scholarship, what I like most is the engaging pedagogy that he provides toward group conversation and faith sharing, welcoming the contribution of each participant. While honoring the legacy of the time-tested *lectio divina*, Binz recrafts this soul-engaging process for busy people in our time, encouraging all to reflect and share our faith—the most likely way to grow it."

Dr. Thomas Groome, *Professor of Theology and Religious Education, Boston College*

"*Threshold Bible Study* is an enriching and enlightening approach to understanding the rich faith which the Scriptures hold for us today. Written in a clear and concise style, *Threshold Bible Study* presents solid contemporary biblical scholarship, offers questions for reflection and/or discussion, and then demonstrates a way to pray from the Scriptures. All these elements work together to offer the reader a wonderful insight into how the sacred texts of our faith can touch our lives in a profound and practical way today. I heartily recommend this series to both individuals and Bible study groups."

Gregory J. Polan, O.S.B., *Conception Abbey, Abbot Primate of the Benedictine Order*

"*Threshold Bible Study* offers solid scholarship and spiritual depth. It can be counted on for lively individual study and prayer, even while it offers spiritual riches to deepen communal conversation and reflection among the people of God."

Dr. Scott Hahn, *Founder and President of the St. Paul Center for Biblical Theology*

"Learning to link our faith with prayer and the Scriptures is an essential task of every Christian. In this work, Stephen J. Binz provides a magnificent opportunity for every Catholic Christian to ponder the faith expressed in the Creed with sacred Scripture and tradition in the context of prayer. If faithfully read and prayed, this scholarly and well-written guide will lead Catholic Christians into an ever-deeper relationship with Jesus Christ and also an appreciation of the gospel's joys and challenges. I recommend it highly."

Rev. Msgr Charles Pope, *Pastor, Holy Comforter–St Cyprian Catholic Church, Washington, DC*

"In this user-friendly work, Catholic scholar Stephen Binz examines in detail the Apostles' Creed and the Nicene Creed as a springboard for evangelization. Such an integrated vital approach to the Bible offers a refreshing and true path to holiness by embracing the paschal mystery in a new way and focusing on the very person of Jesus Christ living in his church."

Bishop David L. Ricken, *Bishop of Green Bay*

"Stephen J. Binz is a consistently outstanding Catholic educator and communicator whose books on the study and application of Scripture have thoroughly enriched my Christian understanding. In our fast-moving, often confusing times, his ability to help us examine and comprehend the truth through all the noise is especially needed and valuable."

Elizabeth Scalia, *writer and speaker, blogger as The Anchoress*

"The books in the *Threshold Bible Study* series by Stephen J. Binz reflect the ideal Catholic approach to biblical interpretation: sound biblical scholarship; a format accessible for lay readership; and a sensitivity to the church's life and spirit. This is what the church means by biblical scholarship at the service of the community of faith."

Donald Senior, C.P., *the late President Emeritus of Catholic Theological Union, member of the Pontifical Biblical Commission*

"The Creed is to the faith what DNA is to the cell. Crammed into it is a vast amount of the revelation given to us by Jesus and poured out in the riches of the word of God. Stephen Binz does a fine job of unpacking the riches tightly wound into this precious gift given by the Holy Spirit to the church."

Mark P. Shea, *author, blogger, and speaker*

How to Use *Threshold Bible Study*

Each book in the *Threshold Bible Study* series is designed to lead you through a new doorway of biblical awareness, to accompany you across a unique threshold of understanding. The characters, places, and images that you encounter in each of these topical studies will help you explore fresh dimensions of your faith and discover richer insights for your spiritual life.

Threshold Bible Study covers biblical themes in depth in a short amount of time. Unlike more traditional Bible studies that treat a biblical book or series of books, *Threshold Bible Study* aims to address specific topics within the entire Bible. The goal is not for you to comprehend everything about each passage, but rather for you to understand what a variety of passages from different books of the Bible reveals about the topic of each study.

Threshold Bible Study offers you an opportunity to explore the entire Bible from the viewpoint of a variety of different themes. The commentary that follows each biblical passage launches your reflection about that passage and helps you begin to see its significance within the context of your contemporary experience. The questions following the commentary challenge you to understand the passage more fully and apply it to your own life. The prayer starter helps conclude your study by integrating learning into your relationship with God.

These studies are designed for maximum flexibility. Each study is presented in a workbook format, with sections for reading, reflecting, writing, discussing, and praying. Space for writing after each question is ideal for personal study and allows group members to prepare in advance for their discussion. The thirty lessons in each topic may be used by an individual over the period of a month, or by a group for six sessions, with lessons to be studied each week before the next group meeting. These studies are ideal for Bible study groups, small Christian communities, adult faith formation, student groups, Sunday school, neighborhood groups, and family reading, as well as for individual learning.

The method of *Threshold Bible Study* is rooted in the classical tradition of *lectio divina*, an ancient yet contemporary means for reading the Scriptures reflectively and prayerfully. Reading and interpreting the text (*lectio*) is followed by reflective meditation on its message (*meditatio*). This reading and reflecting flows into prayer from the heart (*oratio* and *contemplatio*).

This ancient method assures us that Bible study is a matter of both the mind and the heart. It is not just an intellectual exercise to learn more and be able to discuss the Bible with others. It is, more important, a transforming experience. Reflecting on God's word, guided by the Holy Spirit, illumines the mind with wisdom and stirs the heart with zeal.

Following the personal Bible study, *Threshold Bible Study* offers a method for extending *lectio divina* into a weekly conversation with a small group. This communal experience will allow participants to enhance their appreciation of the message and build up a spiritual community (*collatio*). The end result will be to increase not only individual faith but also faithful witness in the context of daily life (*operatio*).

Through the spiritual disciplines of Scripture reading, study, reflection, conversation, and prayer, *Threshold Bible Study* will help you experience God's grace more abundantly and root your life more deeply in Christ. The risen Jesus said: "Listen! I am standing at the door, knocking; if you hear my voice and open the door, I will come in to you and eat with you, and you with me" (Rev 3:20). Listen to the word of God, open the door, and cross the threshold to an unimaginable dwelling with God!

SUGGESTIONS FOR INDIVIDUAL STUDY

- Make your Bible reading a time of prayer. Ask for God's guidance as you read the Scriptures.
- Try to study daily, or as often as possible according to the circumstances of your life.
- Read the Bible passage carefully, trying to understand both its meaning and its personal application as you read. Some persons find it helpful to read the passage aloud.
- Read the passage in another Bible translation. Each version adds to your understanding of the original text.
- Allow the commentary to help you comprehend and apply the scriptural text. The commentary is only a beginning, not the last word, on the meaning of the passage.
- After reflecting on each question, write out your responses. The very act of writing will help you clarify your thoughts, bring new insights, and amplify your understanding.
- As you reflect on your answers, think about how you can live God's word in the context of your daily life.
- Conclude each daily lesson by reading the prayer and continuing with your own prayer from the heart.
- Make sure your reflections and prayers are matters of both the mind and the heart. A true encounter with God's word is always a transforming experience.
- Choose a word or a phrase from the lesson to carry with you throughout the day as a reminder of your encounter with God's life-changing word.
- For additional insights and affirmation, share your learning experience with at least one other person whom you trust. The ideal way to share learning is in a small group that meets regularly.

SUGGESTIONS FOR GROUP STUDY

- Meet regularly; weekly is ideal. Try to be on time and make attendance a high priority for the sake of the group. The average group meets for about an hour.
- Open each session with a prepared prayer, a song, or a reflection. Find some appropriate way to bring the group from the workaday world into a sacred time of graced sharing.
- If you have not been together before, name tags are very helpful as a group begins to become acquainted with the other group members.
- Spend the first session getting acquainted with one another, reading the Introduction aloud, and discussing the questions that follow.
- Appoint a group facilitator to provide guidance to the discussion. The role of facilitator may rotate among members each week. The facilitator simply keeps the discussion on track; each person shares responsibility for the group. There is no need for the facilitator to be a trained teacher.
- Try to study the six lessons on your own during the week. When you have done your own reflection and written your own answers, you will be better prepared to discuss the six scriptural lessons with the group. If you have not had an opportunity to study the passages during the week, meet with the group anyway to share support and insights.
- Participate in the discussion as much as you are able, offering your thoughts, insights, feelings, and decisions. You learn by sharing with others the fruits of your study.
- Be careful not to dominate the discussion. It is important that everyone in the group be offered an equal opportunity to share the results of their work. Try to link what you say to the comments of others so that the group remains on the topic.
- When discussing your own personal thoughts or feelings, use "I" language. Be as personal and honest as appropriate and be very cautious about giving advice to others.

- Listen attentively to the other members of the group so as to learn from their insights. The words of the Bible affect each person in a different way, so a group provides a wealth of understanding for each member.
- Don't fear silence. Silence in a group is as important as silence in personal study. It allows individuals time to listen to the voice of God's Spirit and the opportunity to form their thoughts before they speak.
- Solicit several responses for each question. The thoughts of different people will build on the answers of others and will lead to deeper insights for all.
- Don't fear controversy. Differences of opinions are a sign of a healthy and honest group. If you cannot resolve an issue, continue on, agreeing to disagree. There is probably some truth in each viewpoint.
- Discuss the questions that seem most important for the group. There is no need to cover all the questions in the group session.
- Realize that some questions about the Bible cannot be resolved, even by experts. Don't get stuck on some issue for which there are no clear answers.
- Whatever is said in the group is said in confidence and should be regarded as such.
- Pray as a group in whatever way feels comfortable. Pray for the members of your group throughout the week.

Schedule for Group Study

Session 1: Introduction — Date: ____________________

Session 2: Lessons 1–6 — Date: ____________________

Session 3: Lessons 7–12 — Date: ____________________

Session 4: Lessons 13–18 — Date: ____________________

Session 5: Lessons 19–24 — Date: ____________________

Session 6: Lessons 25–30 — Date: ____________________

One, Holy, Catholic, Apostolic

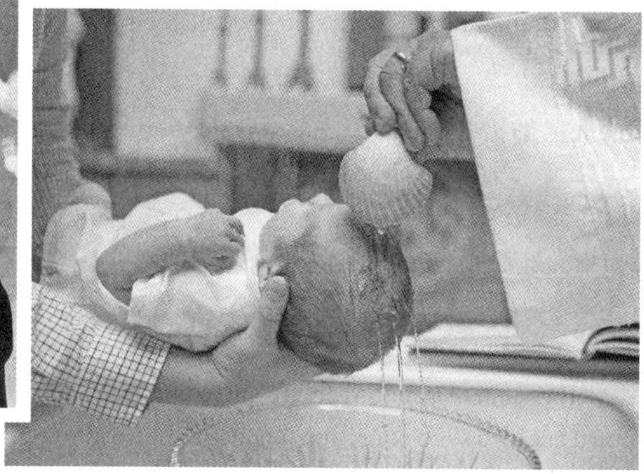

Hold to the standard of sound teaching that you have heard from me, in the faith and love that are in Christ Jesus. Guard the good treasure entrusted to you, with the help of the Holy Spirit living in us.

2 TIMOTHY 1:13–14

The Creed of the Church

When we recite the creed, either in private prayer or in the liturgy of the church, we recite familiar words. These are words that God's people have been proclaiming from the early centuries of Christianity. When we speak these words, we are joining ourselves with fellow believers all around the world, in all the languages of the world, as we profess the faith that unites us in worship of God.

Some recite these words mechanically, without giving much thought to the content and meaning of these ancient statements. They simply reaffirm the beliefs that have become a permanent fixture in their lives. Others, especially those who have newly come into the church, profess the creed as a summary of God's saving work that has transformed their lives. Whether we know these words so well that they have molded our lives in an unconscious way or whether we savor every word with humble gratitude, all of us could better understand these cherished testimonials handed down to us.

Faith is a divine gift. We depend on God's grace to open our minds and move our hearts to convert them to God. Yet, we depend on the human mind and the power of reason to lead us to the edge of faith, to the truth that faith affirms. We also depend on our intellectual capacity to comprehend our faith more fully. Faith naturally seeks understanding, and believers desire to know better the God in whom they have put their faith and to comprehend better what God has revealed.

A more penetrating knowledge of the truths of faith evokes a deeper faith and a more ardent desire for God. A fuller understanding of the mysteries of faith and of God's saving plan leads to a closer union with the Son whom he has sent, the very center of God's revelation. And one cannot believe in the Son, our Lord Jesus Christ, without believing in and sharing in his Spirit. We are able to believe only because of the Holy Spirit at work within us. For, as Paul says, "No one can say 'Jesus is Lord' except by the Holy Spirit" (1 Cor 12:3).

When we proclaim the creed, we realize that we are professing the faith of the church. The church guards the memory of Christ's words, handing on from generation to generation "the faith that was once for all entrusted to the saints" (Jude 3). No one of us believes as much or as well as all of us do communally. It is the church that first believes, and this faith of the church is what supports, nourishes, and sustains the belief of individuals. The church always believes more and better than any one of its members. In this sense, the church is the mother of all believers. As St. Cyprian declared in the third century, "No one can have God as Father who does not have the Church as Mother" (St. Cyprian, *De unit*, 6). The church has constantly professed and defended this one faith, preaching and teaching in the many languages, nations, and cultures of the world, as if with one voice. From East to West and from North to South, the same message and the same way of salvation is made known throughout the whole world.

For the Christian of the twenty-first century, reciting the creed is a countercultural act. In a disposable, consumerist culture, reciting the creed means preserving an ancient tradition. In a world that encourages novelty, we repeat words spoken by people for ages. In a society that avoids commitment, the creed binds people together in covenant with God and one another. In an age that denies absolutes, we claim that there are some truths so important that they must be repeated over and over again.

This study looks at each line of the church's two most important ancient creeds, the Apostles' Creed, from the second century, and the Nicene Creed, from the fourth century. The Apostles' Creed is rightly considered a summary of the apostles' faith and is the baptismal creed of the church of Rome. The Nicene Creed is the expression of faith drawn from the early ecumenical councils of Nicaea and Constantinople (in 325 and 381) and remains the liturgical creed of the great churches of both the East and West.

All the truths proclaimed in the creed are scriptural, and many passages of the Bible pertain to each phrase of the creed. The ones chosen for this study provide an opportunity to reflect on the truths that we profess when we recite the creed. And when we are able to say the creed with understanding and conviction, we can enter more deeply into communion with God the Father, Son, and Holy Spirit, and also with the whole church.

Reflection and Discussion

- What has been my experience of professing the creed? What do I see as the purpose of the creed for my Christian life?

- How do I understand the role of God's grace and my own intellect and will in the act of faith? Why is it important to distinguish between God's role and mine?

The Purpose of the Creed

At the end of Matthew's gospel, Jesus gives his followers the threefold task of the church throughout the ages: 1) "make disciples of all nations," 2) "baptizing them in the name of the Father and of the Son and of the Holy Spirit," and 3) "teaching them to obey everything I have commanded." In its earliest days, the church developed statements of belief to guide these foundational activities. The church's evangelizing mission to the nations was aided by concise statements proclaiming the identity of Jesus and his saving work, many of which are preserved in Paul's speeches and letters. The church's baptizing mission was accompanied by a profession of God as Father, Son, and Holy Spirit. The church's teaching mission was facilitated with summaries of Jesus' instructions and the central truths of the faith. In the ancient church, the creed was instrumental in fulfilling this threefold ministry of the church, and it continues to serve these same purposes today.

Yet, the early church knew that it is not the articulation of the creed that brings people to faith. It is the ongoing presence of Jesus with his church through the Spirit. The last verse of Jesus' instructions ensures his followers of the reality behind the words: "And remember, I am with you always, to the end of the age" In the church's evangelization, sacramental ministry, and ongoing formation of disciples, the presence of Jesus is the heart, but the creed helps the church to carry out the tasks that Jesus commanded with the guidance of the Holy Spirit.

We don't believe in statements of faith, but in those realities they express. Yet, we approach these realities with the help of formulated statements that allow us to express the faith and hand it on, to celebrate it in communal worship, to assimilate it in prayer, and to live it more fully in active witness in the world. Here are some of the most important purposes of the creed:

The creed is a summary of the central truths of Christian faith. It is not intended to be a complete compendium of beliefs expressed in the Bible. It focuses, rather, on the fundamental truths that characterize the life of a Christian believer. As an acorn contains all the elements of a large and verdant tree, the creed condenses into a few words the great faith contained in the Old and New Testaments.

As the authentic and authorized summary of Christian truth, the creed is a symbol of the faith of the whole church. It provides a sign of reception into the church and of membership in the community of faith. By reciting the creed, we state our personal and communal identity. We affirm that we are united in faith with the ancient church and with our fellow believers.

The creed was never meant to be a substitute for personal faith, for a trusting relationship with God. The creed, rather, gives substance to our personal faith. We profess our faith not in the words but in the reality to which they point. Reciting the creed does not make us Christians, but it reminds us of the truths of our salvation and gives us an opportunity to personally affirm them.

The creed is the rule of faith for the Christian life. It supplies a map that lays out the fundamental contours of how the Christian thinks about God and the history of salvation. This map of belief synthesizes the Christian faith and prevents the believer from taking a wrong turn and getting lost. It marks the boundaries of Christian belief and protects the church's essential teachings.

Before the church had a relatively fixed creed, the early theologians referred to the church's communal self-consciousness as the *regula fidei* ("rule of faith"). Although it was articulated in various forms, it presented the essential beliefs inherited from the apostles and passed on through the church. This was understood as the faith which was held "always, everywhere, and by all" (St. Vincent of Lerins, *The Commitorium*, 4, 3) and assured by the Holy Spirit.

This rule of faith, soon to be called a creed, expressed the faith that converts received from the teaching church and were to keep as the standard for their subsequent life. With this rule of faith, Christians were able to interpret the Scriptures according to the mind of the church and test all other doctrines presented to them.

Throughout the church's history, the creed has served as this standard of belief which tests all others and serves the church as the expression of its common faith. In Christian theology, it evaluates theological opinions by testing them for consistency against what has been firmly believed. As a synthesis of the gospel, the creed helps us understand its meaning and guides us in applying the principles of Scripture to the Christian life.

The creed is a renewal of the faith professed at baptism. Since the church's early centuries, those about to be baptized have professed their belief in God the Father, Son, and Holy Spirit and their desire to be immersed in the divine life. This baptismal creed not only states the personal belief of the new Christian in the Trinity but articulates the implications of entering into a new life.

Belief in the Father, Son, and Holy Spirit points to the believer's new relationship, not only with the risen Lord but with God, through the agency of the Holy Spirit. Paul says to the churches in Galatia, "In Christ Jesus you are all children of God through faith. As many of you who were baptized into Christ have clothed yourselves with Christ" (Gal 3:26–27). In baptism we receive the Spirit of the Son, giving us the status of adopted children of God. "God has sent the Spirit of his

Son into our hearts, crying, 'Abba! Father!' So you are no longer a slave but a child, and if a child then also an heir, through God" (Gal 4:6–7).

This baptismal experience is what Christians remember and renew whenever we profess the creed, especially in the Sunday eucharistic assembly. We stand together as God's family, as brothers and sisters of Jesus Christ, through the power of the Holy Spirit. We continue the work that Jesus began, calling God "our Father" and destined to share his inheritance. The words of the creed reaffirm the truths on which we have staked our lives as well as our desire to live the divine life we received at baptism ever more fully.

The creed is the church's liturgical prayer. Professing the creed in public worship reminds us that being a Christian means belonging to the church. It reminds us of the corporate dimensions of faith and helps to correct any unhealthy individualism. By reciting the creed in the context of the Mass, the profession of faith becomes an integral part of the great prayer of thanksgiving we offer to God in the eucharistic liturgy.

Some of the psalms and canticles of the Old Testament give praise to God simply by recounting all the deeds he did on behalf of his people. For this reason, these biblical hymns were part of the worship of God's people in the temple of Jerusalem. Likewise, in the creed we praise God for who he is and for what he has done for us. We worship and glorify God as Father, Son, and Holy Spirit. In addition to being a statement of beliefs, the creed is a prayer addressed to God in which we entrust ourselves to him in gratitude.

In liturgy we give God thanks and entrust ourselves to God together. We proclaim publicly that we are a people defined by the words we profess. Although each person may believe the statements of the creed in slightly different ways or with different degrees of intensity, the worshiping assembly chooses to stand together, united under these truths.

The creed is a springboard for evangelization. The believer has received faith from other people and should desire to hand it on to others. Our love for God and other people and the gratitude we feel for our faith should impel us to speak to others about it. Yet, evangelization is difficult, especially if we haven't thought much about the content of our faith.

The creed is an ideal starting point for the crucial process of consolidating our grasp of the faith. It offers the Christian vision of the world's origins, meaning, and destiny, and it presents God's saving work in a clear and simple statement of beliefs. The creed is not complicated and ambiguous. It requires no hidden knowledge or superior intellect, and it can be affirmed and understood by children as well as adults.

The creed focuses on what unites believers rather than on what divides them. It thus encourages the kind of ecumenical understanding called for by the church today. The statements of the creed establish strong and clear boundaries for Christian belief, but those boundaries do not become barriers that exclude those who might not yet be able to accept other points of doctrine.

As we study the ancient confessions of the church, we develop our ability to express our faith in tune with the received wisdom of the ages. In our confused and creedless age, which hesitates to acknowledge any unchanging truth, our testimony to the ancient wisdom of the church and the guidance of God's Spirit can offer refreshment and confidence to those seeking the unconditional truth and love of our saving God. By articulating our own experience of faith in union with the words of the creed, we cultivate Christian testimony worthy of the Lord to whom we witness.

Reflection and Discussion

- In what ways does the Creed enable the church to carry out the basic tasks given to it by the Risen Lord?

- In what ways does the creed broaden my vision of the world and offer me a clearer sense of my place within it?

The Development of the Creed

Since its earliest days, the church has expressed and handed on its faith in concise statements. These first took the form of brief assertions about the identity of Jesus, much like the response of Peter when Jesus asked who he is: "You are the Messiah, the Son of the living God" (Matt 16:16). Probably the earliest form of the Christian creed is found in Paul's letters: "Jesus is Lord!" This is the essence of Christian belief, distinguishing it from all other religions.

As these statements of faith developed, they became affirmations of faith in the Trinity—Father, Son, and Holy Spirit. The gospel, which tells of the Son of God coming to earth, dying to redeem us, sending the Spirit to his church, and finally coming in judgment, all to fulfill the saving will of the Father, cannot be expressed without speaking in a Trinitarian way about the work of the Father, Son, and Holy Spirit. Even though Paul blessed the church in Corinth with the words "The grace of the Lord Jesus Christ, the love of God, and the communion of the Holy Spirit be with all of you" (2 Cor 13:13), the understanding of the Trinity is a mystery of faith that can only gradually be understood. Although the one God is manifested as three persons throughout Scripture, it took a while for the church to fully articulate this belief.

These expressions of the faith of the church are called creeds because they usually begin with the Latin word *credo* ("I believe"). The earliest form of these creeds was interrogative: "Do you believe in God the Father… Do you believe in Jesus the Son… Do you believe in the Holy Spirit…?" These questions were asked of new believers during the celebration of baptism before each of the three immersions or pourings of water over the head. Through this baptismal creed, new Christians made their first public declaration of faith.

As the creeds developed in the early centuries, they expanded beyond an affirmation of God the Father, Son, and Holy Spirit and God's saving work. Points of doctrine were added to the Trinitarian outline to clarify the church's beliefs in contrast to ideas that seemed the greatest threats to Christian faith. For example, church councils added the phrase "all things visible and invisible" to clarify the scope of God's creation, in contrast to the heretical view that God is opposed to the material world. Many phrases were also added to the saving acts of God the Son to clarify his relationship to the Father. In contrast to those who were teaching that Jesus was human and later adopted by God as his Son, at either his baptism or his resurrection, the creeds affirmed that he is "consubstantial with the Father." In this way, the creed develops implications of the experiences and convictions present in Christianity from its beginnings.

As Christianity became an increasingly worldwide church, it experienced the need to establish more coherence among its many local communities. Because it faced deep internal divisions concerning the nature of Christ and salvation, many of the early Fathers of the church desired to establish a norm for "orthodoxy" (right teaching). Through their writings, the creed expanded to meet challenges to the church's unity as they occurred in the first three centuries. While the creed is historically conditioned in this sense, expressing points of doctrine that seemed to be most threatened at the time, it nevertheless succinctly states the permanent beliefs of the church and is an instrument of its unity.

The creed is not the collected thoughts of isolated individuals. It is, rather, the beliefs of the corporate body of Christ. It was written collectively, in ecumenical councils. And those who professed the creed in the church's early centuries rightly believed that it expresses the truths of the inspired Scriptures as given to the church. For this reason, the creed is not something an individual can believe in isolation from the church. The creed has a unifying and communal character. It is not individual opinion; it is the time-proven faith of the church.

The way the creed developed in history demonstrates that Christianity is most definitely not an individualistic religion. It is personal, yes, and experienced in the heart of individuals, but it is not individualistic. For, individualism creates splintering and division, but the church is characterized by its stable foundation on the apostles and its unity in the Holy Spirit. The creed is simply what Christians believe. All who wish to follow Christ must join with others who also believe what has been handed down through the centuries in the church.

When catechumens were prepared for baptism in the early centuries, they were taught the creed toward the end of their preparation. The creed was "handed over" to them as a symbol of faith, an expression of the communal faith shared by the community into which they were being initiated. After several sessions of explanation, they then would hand it back by reciting the creed in the presence of the bishop and the congregation, affirming the faith into which they would be baptized. This ritual is still practiced today in many parishes and is a powerful way of affirming the communal faith of the whole church handed on through the ages.

When we profess the creed, we are declaring ourselves as part of that countless multitude throughout the centuries who have found their identity in the same gospel and the same community of faith. This multitude includes brave martyrs, great theologians, noble saints, and selfless missionaries—all of whom share the tradition given to us by the apostles and handed on in the church. To believe is to belong. Baptized into Jesus Christ, we have entered a community of faith whose existence stretches back to the upper room in Jerusalem. We have become a member of his body, the church, which uses this creed to express its faith. By studying it, we realize that we are united with those countless men and women down through the centuries who recited these words at their baptism and have professed this faith at the Sunday Eucharist. We share that same personal faith in God as Father, Son, and Holy Spirit, and we share the same words to express it.

Reflection and discussion

- In what ways is my appreciation for the creed enhanced by understanding its historical developments?

- What would I like to understand better about the beliefs of the church in the course of this study?

Prayer

Lord our God, the beginning and the end of all creation, send your Holy Spirit to guide, encourage, and enlighten me as I begin this study of the church's creed. As I examine the biblical foundations of the church's creed, deepen my Christian faith and help me appreciate the living tradition in which I live. May these Scriptures probe my heart, move me to new insights, and transform my motives and actions. Draw me ever closer to Jesus and form me into his missionary disciple.

THE APOSTLES' CREED

I believe in God,
the Father almighty,
Creator of heaven and earth,
and in Jesus Christ, his only Son,
our Lord,
who was conceived by the
Holy Spirit,
born of the Virgin Mary,
suffered under Pontius Pilate,
was crucified, died and was buried;
he descended into hell;
on the third day he rose again from
the dead;
he ascended into heaven,
and is seated at the right hand of
God the Father almighty;
from there he will come to judge the
living and the dead.
I believe in the Holy Spirit,
the holy catholic Church,
the communion of saints,
the forgiveness of sins,
the resurrection of the body,
and life everlasting. Amen.

THE NICENE CREED

I believe in one God,
the Father almighty,
maker of heaven and earth,
of all things visible and invisible.
I believe in one Lord Jesus Christ,
the Only Begotten Son of God,
born of the Father before all ages.
God from God, Light from Light,
true God from true God,
begotten, not made, consubstantial
with the Father;
through him all things were made.
For us men and for our salvation
he came down from heaven,
and by the Holy Spirit was incarnate
of the Virgin Mary,
and became man.
For our sake he was crucified under
Pontius Pilate,
he suffered death and was buried,
and rose again on the third day
in accordance with the Scriptures.
He ascended into heaven
and is seated at the right hand of
the Father.
He will come again in glory
to judge the living and the dead
and his kingdom will have no end.
I believe in the Holy Spirit, the Lord,
the giver of life,
who proceeds from the Father and
the Son,
who with the Father and the Son is
adored and glorified,
who has spoken through
the prophets.
I believe in one, holy, catholic and
apostolic Church.
I confess one Baptism for the
forgiveness of sins
and I look forward to the
resurrection of the dead
and the life of the world to
come. Amen.

SUGGESTIONS FOR FACILITATORS, GROUP SESSION 1

1. If the group is meeting for the first time, or if there are newcomers joining the group, it is helpful to provide nametags.

2. Distribute the books to the members of the group.

3. You may want to ask the participants to introduce themselves and tell the group a bit about themselves.

4. Ask one or more of these introductory questions:
    - What drew you to join this group?
    - What is your biggest fear in beginning this Bible study?
    - How is beginning this study like a "threshold" for you?

5. You may want to pray this prayer as a group:
   Come upon us, Holy Spirit, to enlighten and guide us as we begin this study of the creed. You inspired the biblical authors to express your word as manifested to the people of Israel and most fully in the life of Jesus. Motivate us each day to read the Scriptures and deepen our understanding and love for these sacred texts. Bless us during this session and throughout the coming week with the fire of your love.

6. Read the Introduction aloud, pausing at each question for discussion. Group members may wish to write down the insights of the group as each question is discussed. Encourage several members of the group to respond to each question.

7. Don't feel compelled to finish the complete Introduction during the session. It is better to allow sufficient time to talk about the questions raised than to rush to the end. Group members may read any remaining sections on their own after the group meeting.

8. Instruct group members to read the first six lessons on their own during the six days before the next group meeting. They should write out their own answers to the questions as preparation for next week's group discussion.

9. Fill in the date for each group meeting under "Schedule for Group Study."

10. Conclude by praying aloud together the prayer at the end of the Introduction.

LESSON 1 | SESSION 2

No distrust made him waver concerning the promise of God, but [Abraham] grew strong in his faith as he gave glory to God, being fully convinced that God was able to do what he had promised.

ROMANS 4:20–21

I Believe

HEBREWS 11:8–16 [8]*By faith Abraham obeyed when he was called to set out for*
a place that he was to receive as an inheritance; and he set out, not knowing where
he was going. [9]*By faith he stayed for a time in the land he had been promised, as*
in a foreign land, living in tents, as did Isaac and Jacob, who were heirs with him
of the same promise. [10]*For he looked forward to the city that has foundations,*
whose architect and builder is God. [11]*By faith he received power of procreation,*
even though he was too old—and Sarah herself was barren—because he consid-
ered him faithful who had promised. [12]*Therefore from one person, and this one as*
good as dead, descendants were born, "as many as the stars of heaven and as the
innumerable grains of sand by the seashore."

[13]*All of these died in faith without having received the promises, but from a*
distance they saw and greeted them. They confessed that they were strangers and
foreigners on the earth, [14]*for people who speak in this way make it clear that they*
are seeking a homeland. [15]*If they had been thinking of the land that they had left*
behind, they would have had opportunity to return. [16]*But as it is, they desire a*
better country, that is, a heavenly one. Therefore God is not ashamed to be called
their God; indeed, he has prepared a city for them.

ROMANS 4:13–25 [13]*For the promise that he would inherit the world did not*
come to Abraham or to his descendants through the law but through the righ-
teousness of faith. [14]*If it is the adherents of the law who are to be the heirs, faith is*

null and the promise is void. [15]*For the law brings wrath; but where there is no law,*
neither is there violation.

[16]*For this reason it depends on faith, in order that the promise may rest on grace*
and be guaranteed to all his descendants, not only to the adherents of the law but
also to those who share the faith of Abraham (for he is the father of all of us, [17]*as*
it is written, "I have made you the father of many nations")—in the presence of
the God in whom he believed, who gives life to the dead and calls into existence the
things that do not exist. [18]*Hoping against hope, he believed that he would become*
"the father of many nations," according to what was said, "So numerous shall your
descendants be." [19]*He did not weaken in faith when he considered his own body,*
which was already as good as dead (for he was about a hundred years old), or when
he considered the barrenness of Sarah's womb. [20]*No distrust made him waver con-*
cerning the promise of God, but he grew strong in his faith as he gave glory to God,
[21]*being fully convinced that God was able to do what he had promised.* [22]*Therefore*
his faith "was reckoned to him as righteousness." [23]*Now the words, "it was reckoned*
to him," were written not for his sake alone, [24]*but for ours also. It will be reckoned to*
us who believe in him who raised Jesus our Lord from the dead, [25]*who was handed*
over to death for our trespasses and was raised for our justification.

Faith is a response of the whole person to God, characterized by trust, obedience, and loyalty. Among the lives portrayed in Scripture, Abraham is the finest exemplar of faith. The accounts of his life in Genesis demonstrate that he believed in God and thus became the ancestor of all believers. Both the writer of Hebrews and Paul highlight the depths of Abraham's faith and propose him as a model for Christian believers. As a man of faith, he trusted God's promises to him, he obeyed God's call to him, and he was loyal to God when the circumstances of his life made God's promises seem impossible to fulfill.

Abraham was sent out by God from his homeland, and his whole life would be a journey of faith. Abraham obeyed and departed, not knowing where he was going, trusting only that God would lead him to the land he promised to give him as an inheritance. He left the known and familiar and entrusted his future to God. Reaching the promised land, he continued to journey in tents, like a stranger in a foreign land. Though Sarah was barren and Abraham was probably impotent, God promised Abraham that he would have innumerable descendants. Abraham and Sarah trusted in the faithfulness of God and received the power of procreation, when all seemed humanly impossible.

Living nearly two millennia after Abraham, Paul calls Abraham the "father of many nations," the "father of all of us" (Rom 4:16, 18). Abraham's offspring would surpass the boundaries of Israel and fill the whole earth. His heirs would be all people who come to know the God of Abraham and walk by faith. This is the God "who gives life to the dead and calls into existence the things that do not exist." This same God of the impossible is also Paul's God. And Paul convinces us that this same creating and redeeming God is our God, too, the God "who raised Jesus our Lord from the dead."

The only response to such a God is faith. Trying to earn the favor of such a God or merit his blessings would be foolish. Because Abraham opened his life to God in trust and obedience, God transformed the obstacles Abraham encountered into possibilities for something beyond his dreams. For Paul, Abraham is the key to understanding the meaning of God's grace and our appropriate response in faith. Abraham's faith was not an easy choice; it was a constant struggle. He questioned God, doubted God, pleaded with God. And through this struggle his faith became deeper and stronger.

A man of faith, Abraham continued to journey toward the unseen and unknown, acting on the basis of God's promises alone. Yet, the promises and blessings experienced by Abraham, as wonderful as they were, were only a shadow of the transcendent reality still to come. The writer of Hebrews says that Abraham knew that his true "homeland" was not to be found in his earthly life. The promised land was only a tract of real estate on the eastern shore of the Mediterranean. Abraham looked forward to "a better country," to "the city that has foundations," a stable and lasting city "whose architect and builder is God."

Abraham's faith was not a passive waiting on God; it was a lively obedience motivated by God's trustworthiness. As James explains in his letter, Abraham's faith was brought to completion by his works (James 2:21–24). God's promises, the things hoped for, though not yet seen, are a powerful motivator for people of faith. Like Abraham, we live our lives as pilgrims, not always knowing where we are going but led by God's promises. The journey is challenging and risky and never confined to a single generation. Abraham, the father of all believers, has gone ahead of us to show us the way to live in faith.

Reflection and discussion

- Since Abraham's faith has made him "the father of us all," in what ways is Abraham a model of faith for me? What does it mean to me to say, "I believe"?

- Read James 2:18–24 to better understand that a life of obedient works must accompany faith. In what ways does Abraham demonstrate the life of works accompanying his faith?

- Since God's power working through faith within us can do more than we can hope or imagine, how is God working within me today to prompt me to act on faith?

Prayer

God of our ancestors, you called Abraham and his descendants to believe your word and trust in your promises. Give me faith to believe in you as the God of the impossible, the one who creates out of nothing and raises the dead to life.

Ever since the creation of the world his eternal power and divine nature, invisible though they are, have been understood and seen through the things he has made. ROMANS 1:20

I Believe in God

WISDOM 13:1–9 1*For all people who were ignorant of God were foolish by nature;*
and they were unable from the good things that are seen to know
the one who exists,
nor did they recognize the artisan while paying heed to his works;
2*but they supposed that either fire or wind or swift air,*
or the circle of the stars, or turbulent water,
or the luminaries of heaven were the gods that rule the world.
3*If through delight in the beauty of these things people assumed them to be gods,*
let them know how much better than these is their Lord,
for the author of beauty created them.
4*And if people were amazed at their power and working,*
let them perceive from them
how much more powerful is the one who formed them.
5*For from the greatness and beauty of created things*
comes a corresponding perception of their Creator.
6*Yet these people are little to be blamed,*
for perhaps they go astray
while seeking God and desiring to find him.
7*For while they live among his works, they keep searching,*
and they trust in what they see, because the things that are seen are beautiful.
8*Yet again, not even they are to be excused;*
9*for if they had the power to know so much*

that they could investigate the world,
how did they fail to find sooner the Lord of these things?

ROMANS 1:19–22 [19]*For what can be known about God is plain to them, because God has shown it to them.* [20]*Ever since the creation of the world his eternal power and divine nature, invisible though they are, have been understood and seen through the things he has made. So they are without excuse;* [21]*for though they knew God, they did not honor him as God or give thanks to him, but they became futile in their thinking, and their senseless minds were darkened.* [22]*Claiming to be wise, they became fools.*

The sage who composed the book of Wisdom reflects on the foolishness of those who admire the good things of the world but are unable to know God. Seeing the goodness, diversity, order, and beauty of creation ought to lead a person to knowledge of their source, the Creator and cause of it all. The sage calls this first cause and primary source of all things "the one who exists." This term for God is both the name by which God revealed himself to Moses (Exodus 3:14) and also the term describing the deity in Greek philosophy. But although Greek thought was able to understand God as transcendent being, it did not proceed to describe God as Creator. Fortunately, God's revelation to the Israelites led to the understanding that "the one who exists" is the Creator of all that is, the transcendent deity on whom the universe is totally dependent. While marveling at the works of creation, they were able to recognize "the artisan," the personal Creator who made them all.

Human beings have a natural attraction to beauty. This innate longing for what is beautiful can be cultivated and refined by contemplative reflection on the experience of beauty. Much of the biblical literature, especially in the Psalms and wisdom literature, is this kind of thoughtful reflection about the attractiveness of the world. Stars, sunrises, rainbows, mountains, trees, and flowers are praised for their beauty. Often, however, people in the ancient world made the mistake of worshiping the alluring creation rather than the Creator. They assumed the sun, moon, stars, fiery storm, or turbulent sea to be gods who ruled the world. As the sage describes this tendency, "Through delight in the beauty of these things people assumed them to be gods" (Wis 13:3).

People today sometimes draw similar conclusions because of the attractive power of natural beauty. Various expressions of pantheism identify God with the world and the world with God. The biblical writers, however, always express the transcendence of God as distinct from the world of created reality, but at the same time insist that God can be known through observing the power, beauty, order, and goodness of the world. This sacramental view of the world insists that nature is not God, but that the natural world points us to the existence of God: "From the greatness and beauty of created things comes a corresponding perception of their Creator" (Wis 13:5).

Paul expresses the same understanding in his letter to the Romans, insisting that God's "eternal power and divine nature," though invisible, can be discerned through the things that God has made (Rom 1:20). Works of art bear the imprint of the mind and heart of the artist. Creation bears the imprint of "the author of beauty," and through its beauty humanity experiences something of the Creator's wisdom, power, and goodness.

In English, the words "I believe" can have many different meanings. We can hold a belief that something is true without letting that belief matter for our lives. Sometimes the creed is treated simply as a set of beliefs that amount to no more than strongly held opinions. Yet, the faith expressed in the creed is much more. The faith expressed in the creedal expression "I believe in" corresponds to the New Testament understanding of faith. The term *pistis* ("faith" in Greek) indicates the entire human response to God, including belief, trust, fidelity, and obedience. It is a response of the whole person, not just the intellect.

During the profession of the creed, we do not say "I believe that…" but rather "I believe in…." This level of faith is possible only toward a person rather than an intellectual truth. If a child is willing to jump off a ledge into the arms of her father, we know that the child is willing because she "believes in" her father. She trusts him and is willing to stake her life on him. When we profess "I believe in God," we are not merely saying that we believe that God exists. We are not expressing our opinion that there is a God or that, after due consideration, we have come to the conclusion that God exists, or even that we are absolutely convinced that God exists. Rather, we are expressing our trust in God, our willingness to place our lives in his hands, our desire to surrender our lives to him.

Certainly believing "in" God requires believing also "that" there is a God. But this is not the main emphasis of our words. "I believe in God" means that it is in this God that we live and believe. This kind of faith means that God is both the foundation and the context of all that we believe. The same is true of the entire creed. There are three persons "in" whom we believe: the Father almighty, his Son Jesus Christ, and the Holy Spirit. In this sense, it is only "in" God that we believe. In the context of this belief in God, we believe "that" God is the maker of heaven and earth, "that" Jesus died and rose again, "that" the Holy Spirit spoke through the prophets. But our primary focus is not our beliefs but the God in whom we believe.

Faith in God and in the truths of God's revelation is quite different from the kind of knowledge we gain through the scientific method. The realities of faith cannot be verified by observable facts. These divine realities engage us on a deep and personal level. In the face of these divine realities, we cannot remain aloof and objective. They demand our personal response and our commitment. "I believe in God" cannot be a casual statement. Rather, it impacts our stance toward everything that exists. It affirms that reality does not consist only in what we can see and touch, measure and calculate. There is mystery at the heart of the world, mystery that suggests its presence in every single thing that we can see, hear, feel, taste, and smell in the world. Belief in God is the intuitive response of human creatures to the world, the natural assumption made by nearly every human who has inhabited the earth. It affirms that the world is a marvelous gift. Since the world is freely given and not simply "there," it can be studied with wonder, contemplated in awe, and celebrated with joy.

Reflection and discussion

- Why is beauty so attractive to us? What does the title "author of beauty" (Wis 13:3) tell me about God?

- In what ways is the quality of the statement "I believe in" different from the quality of the statement "I believe that"? How is the truth that we express in the creed different from scientific truth?

- Philosophers and spiritual masters have expressed a variety of intimations of God's existence: the beauty of the world, the workings of the human heart, the goodness of people, the mystery of love, etc. What are some experiences that lead me to affirm a belief in God?

- Because belief in God impacts our stance toward everything that exists, refusal to acknowledge God as giver and creation as gift can result in individualism, greed, idolatry, consumerism, addiction, and boredom. What is the impact of my deepening belief on my relationship to the world?

- As in biblical times, we often replace our adoration of the true God with worship of the things God has made. What are some of the idols in today's world? How can I replace one of the idols I worship with adoration of God?

Prayer

Author of Beauty, you are the source and cause of all that exists. Give me the insight to see your eternal power and creative love in the things you have made. As I reflect on the beauty you have made, lead me to worship you as the Creator and Lord of all.

LESSON 3 SESSION 2

Turn to me and be saved, all the ends of the earth!
For I am God, and there is no other. ISAIAH 45:22

I Believe in One God

DEUTERONOMY 6:4–9 4 *Hear, O Israel: The Lord is our God, the Lord alone.*
5 *You shall love the Lord your God with all your heart, and with all your soul, and*
with all your might. 6 *Keep these words that I am commanding you today in your*
heart. 7 *Recite them to your children and talk about them when you are at home*
and when you are away, when you lie down and when you rise. 8 *Bind them as a*
sign on your hand, fix them as an emblem on your forehead, 9 *and write them on*
the doorposts of your house and on your gates.

ISAIAH 45:22–25 22 *Turn to me and be saved,*
all the ends of the earth!
For I am God, and there is no other.
23 *By myself I have sworn,*
from my mouth has gone forth in righteousness
a word that shall not return:
"To me every knee shall bow,
every tongue shall swear."

24 *Only in the Lord, it shall be said of me,*
are righteousness and strength;
all who were incensed against him
shall come to him and be ashamed.
25 *In the Lord all the offspring of Israel*
shall triumph and glory.

In biblical times, the people of Israel professed belief in one God, sharply distinguishing them from the surrounding nations who proclaimed many gods. Today, belief in God must be professed in the face of atheism. Formerly, the world believed in too many gods. Nowadays, many in the world believe in no god at all. The Jewish and Christian confidence in one God is no less essential today than it was in ancient times.

The earliest biblical writings indicate that Israel's profession of the Lord alone developed from their understanding of YHWH as superior to the gods of all other peoples. For example, the psalmist's prayer, "For the Lord is a great God, and a great King above all gods" (Psalm 95:3), suggests a belief that God stands as the first among many gods. Because the Israelites were freed from Egypt and conquered the land of Canaan, they viewed their God as triumphant over the deities of the Egyptians and Canaanites.

Later reflection led to the understanding that YHWH alone is God, the one God of the whole world and of all peoples. The later parts of Isaiah affirm monotheism with unambiguous clarity: "For I am God, and there is no other" (Isa 45:22). God's salvation is not directed toward Israel alone, but peoples from "all the ends of the earth" can turn to the one true God. The divine choice of Israel is not an inward-looking privilege; rather, it is part of a universal drama that will be completed when "every knee shall bow, every tongue shall swear" to the Creator and Redeemer of the world (Isa 45:23).

The Shema Yisrael (Deut 6:4–9) was the touchstone for the faith and life of ancient Israel and is the prayer offered by Jewish believers every morning and evening. These primary words are meant to shape their daily conduct and their interior direction. The command of the Shema urges believers to discover afresh in every new experience the implications of holding the one God at the center of their being.

The opening imperative may be translated as "The Lord is our God, the Lord alone," or as "The Lord is our God, the Lord is one." This ambiguity of meaning challenges the believer to trust in both the uniqueness and the oneness of God. Yet, truly these attributes of God are two sides of the same coin. "The Lord is one" professes that God is totally faithful and consistent, that God's purposes are not divided in any way. "The Lord alone" proclaims that the loyalties of God's people are not divided, that they have no other God but the Lord.

The command to love God with all your heart, soul, and might indicates covenant fidelity. It is expressed in loyalty and service that flows from a personal, intimate, trusting relationship with God. Israel demonstrated this love toward the Lord in authentic worship and obedience to the Torah. This love calls for total commitment. God's covenant partners must love him wholeheartedly, with all their being, with their whole selves. The oneness and uniqueness of the Lord God must be matched by the oneness and totality of his people's devotion.

Following the command to "hear" these words and to "love" God with your whole being, a rapid series of verbs follows: "Keep these words…recite them…talk about them…bind them…fix them…write them" (Deut 6:6–9). Fixing the words of the Shema on one's forehead and hand means binding them into one's own life. Writing the words on one's doorposts means making them vital for one's home and family. Inscribing them on the city gates, the place of civic life, means making them crucial for society. In time, these internal attitudes of the heart began to be expressed with external religious symbols. These are the ways that God's people flavored the whole of life with conscious attention to God.

Understanding that there is only one absolute that undergirds all reality assures us that there is an order and a purpose to the universe. In the midst of the multiple and conflicting claims of our lives, the knowledge that there is only one ground of all existence prevents our lives from seeming too chaotic and unmanageable. Our full and ultimate allegiance is to God alone. All other loyalties that might divide our time and focus are only secondary. The center of all being, value, and meaning is the God who is one, consistent, and faithful.

Reflection and discussion

- In what ways does belief in one God, the ultimate source and sole foundation for all existence, make a difference in my understanding of life's meaning and purpose?

- The Shema insists that children be taught to know and love God through repetition, reminders, and discussion. What method of learning does Moses seem to suggest in Deuteronomy 6:7–9?

- How does my deepening love for God—with all my heart, soul, and might—influence my motivation for worshiping God and my desire to follow God's law?

- In what ways can external religious symbols promote internal attitudes of the heart? What are some examples in my life?

Prayer

Creator and Lord, you are the one and only God. Give me a heartfelt love for you and a genuine desire to do your will in all things. Bestow on me the grace to love you completely in my personal life, my family life, and my communal life.

LESSON 4 SESSION 2

“Do you not believe that I am in the Father and the Father is in me? The words that I say to you I do not speak on my own; but the Father who dwells in me does his works.” JOHN 14:10

The Father Almighty

JOHN 14:1–11 1*“Do not let your hearts be troubled. Believe in God, believe also in me.* 2*In my Father’s house there are many dwelling places. If it were not so, would I have told you that I go to prepare a place for you?* 3*And if I go and prepare a place for you, I will come again and will take you to myself, so that where I am, there you may be also.* 4*And you know the way to the place where I am going.”* 5*Thomas said to him, “Lord, we do not know where you are going. How can we know the way?”* 6*Jesus said to him, “I am the way, and the truth, and the life. No one comes to the Father except through me.* 7*If you know me, you will know my Father also. From now on you do know him and have seen him.”*

8*Philip said to him, “Lord, show us the Father, and we will be satisfied.”* 9*Jesus said to him, “Have I been with you all this time, Philip, and you still do not know me? Whoever has seen me has seen the Father. How can you say, ‘Show us the Father’?* 10*Do you not believe that I am in the Father and the Father is in me? The words that I say to you I do not speak on my own; but the Father who dwells in me does his works.* 11*Believe me that I am in the Father and the Father is in me; but if you do not, then believe me because of the works themselves.*

ACTS 17:22–28 22*Then Paul stood in front of the Areopagus and said, “Athenians, I see how extremely religious you are in every way.* 23*For as I went through the city and looked carefully at the objects of your worship, I found among them an altar with the inscription, ‘To an unknown god.’ What therefore you worship as unknown, this I proclaim to you.* 24*The God who made the world and everything in it, he who is Lord* *of heaven and earth, does not live in shrines made by human hands,* [25]*nor is he served by human hands, as though he needed anything, since he himself gives to all mortals life and breath and all things.* [26]*From one ancestor he made all nations to inhabit the whole earth, and he allotted the times of their existence and the boundaries of the places where they would live,* [27]*so that they would search for God and perhaps grope for him and find him—though indeed he is not far from each one of us.* [28]*For 'In him we live and move and have our being'; as even some of your own poets have said,*

'For we too are his offspring.'"

When we describe God as the Father, we look beyond any understandings of God as merely an impersonal being or force. In the Old Testament, Moses described God as "your father, who created you" (Deut 32:6) and Israel is called God's "firstborn son" (Exod 4:22). God is also revealed as Father of Israel's anointed king (2 Sam 7:14). Yet, it is not until the life and teachings of Jesus Christ that God is fully made known as the Father. Jesus addressed God as "Abba" (dear Father) and described God as "my Father" throughout his life. Jesus revealed God as eternally Father by his relationship to his only Son who, reciprocally, is Son only in relationship to his Father.

In Jesus' farewell discourse, he urges his disciples, "Believe in God, believe also in me," so that they may not be discouraged (John 14:1). He assures them that one of the purposes of his leaving is to prepare a place for them among the many places for dwelling in his Father's house. The image suggests that in God's household, there is abundant space and family closeness for all those who follow Jesus. As Son of the Father, Jesus establishes his disciples as members of the Father's household and makes his own home a permanent, eternal residence for them.

When Jesus tells his disciples that they already know the way to the Father's home, Thomas replies that they know neither the place where Jesus is going nor how to get there. Jesus responds by telling Thomas that he himself is the road to the Father: "I am the way, and the truth, and the life. No one comes to the Father except through me" (John 14:6). Jesus is the way to experience the very essence of truth and the fullness of life. He is going to the Father, whose love forever defines the meaning of being home.

When Jesus tells his disciples that they already know the Father and have seen him, Philip is confused because he knows that the Father is transcendent, the one whom even Moses was not allowed to see (Exod 33:20). As Philip asks to be shown the Father, Jesus responds, "Whoever has seen me has seen the Father... Believe me that I am in the Father and the Father is in me" (John 14:8–11). The union between the Father and the Son is so intimate that knowing Jesus and seeing his work reveals the transcendent God.

The responses of Thomas and Philip to the teachings of Jesus indicate that they do not yet understand the oneness of the Father and the Son or how they themselves will enter by faith into that wondrous flow of life between the Father and the Son. The full understanding of this relationship and their participation in this divine life will come only through the gift of the Holy Spirit. Through the Spirit, disciples of Jesus will become adopted sons and daughters of the world's Creator and call upon him as "our Father."

The Almighty God, who is also our Father, is the one God of all peoples. As Paul teaches the philosophers and political figures of Athens, he explains that the many temples and statues of the city represent a genuine search for the divine and an expression of the human impulse to worship. Their "unknown god" is "Lord of heaven and earth" (Acts 17:22, 24). Paul demonstrates how Jerusalem can speak to Athens, how divine revelation can dialogue with human reason. He quotes Greek writers as legitimate conversation partners in approaching the truth of the gospel. However, speculative thinking can move people only to the borders of faith. Human beings remain unsatisfied and unfulfilled until we enter into a relationship with the almighty Creator. The God in whom "we live and move and have our being" (Acts 17:28) is the living and personal God revealed in the Scriptures of Israel and in the life, death, and resurrection of Jesus Christ. Before this God all people must repent, and in him all must come to believe.

Reflection and discussion

- What are the issues that are perplexing Thomas and Philip while Jesus teaches them? In what ways do I also struggle with these issues of understanding and belief?

- What are some of the positive signs that Paul saw and heard in Athens? In what ways do these express the searching and longing of people today?

- Paul's work in Athens is an example of the ways that human reason and divine faith can dialogue. How can Paul serve as a model for the ways that Christians can dialogue with other religions and with the secular world today?

- Realizing that God reveals his presence in the longings of the human heart, what one person could I bring closer to God today through his or her own natural longing for transcendence?

Prayer

Almighty Father, Lord of heaven and earth, you have instilled in all people a natural yearning and desire for you. Help me to recognize the restless probing of my own heart and show me ways to seek out the confused hearts of others who are searching for you.

Have you not known? Have you not heard? The Lord is the everlasting God, the Creator of the ends of the earth. ISAIAH 40:28

Maker of Heaven and Earth

ISAIAH 40:25–28 25*To whom then will you compare me,*
or who is my equal? says the Holy One.
26*Lift up your eyes on high and see:*
Who created these?
He who brings out their host and numbers them,
calling them all by name;
because he is great in strength,
mighty in power,
not one is missing.

27*Why do you say, O Jacob,*
and speak, O Israel,
"My way is hidden from the Lord,
and my right is disregarded by my God"?
28*Have you not known? Have you not heard?*
The Lord is the everlasting God,
the Creator of the ends of the earth.
He does not faint or grow weary;
his understanding is unsearchable.

PSALM 8:3–9 3*When I look at your heavens, the work of your fingers,*
the moon and the stars that you have established;
4*what are human beings that you are mindful of them,*
mortals that you care for them?

5 *Yet you have made them a little lower than God,*
and crowned them with glory and honor.
6 *You have given them dominion over the works of your hands;*
you have put all things under their feet,
7 *all sheep and oxen,*
and also the beasts of the field,
8 *the birds of the air, and the fish of the sea,*
whatever passes along the paths of the seas.
9 *O Lord, our Sovereign,*
how majestic is your name in all the earth!

The reality that God is the eternal cause of the cosmos, the Creator of heaven and earth, is expressed in a variety of ways in Scripture. The prophets and psalms proclaim the creative power of God and the wondrous beauty and goodness of the things God has made. The first account of creation in Genesis is a piece of liturgical poetry expressing God's causing all things to come into existence with the power of his word (Gen 1). The second creation account describes God as a creative sculptor, forming the human from the clay and breathing into his nostrils to give him life. God then planted a garden and formed from the ground all the animals of the field and birds of the air (Gen 2:7, 19). The book of Job describes God as a master builder, carefully laying the world's foundation and cornerstone, then causing everything to come into existence with his mighty command (Job 38). The Psalms praise God's loving care for the earth and describe how God is continually creating the world and holding all things in existence (Ps 104). These Scriptures convince us that God causes the world to be—not once long ago, but at every moment.

Clearly, the Bible and the creed refrain from advocating any particular theory about how God caused the world to come into being or about the way God sustains all things in existence. For this reason, the biblical and creedal truths about God as Creator are compatible with any number of scientific explanations. Science can propose theories about *how* the world came to be, and revelation shows us *why* the world came to be. Not only are the theories of evolution and an expanding universe compatible with biblical truth, they actually do more honor to the biblical understanding of creation as a continuing process sustained by God than does a literalistic understanding of

Scripture. Treating the Bible as a source of scientific knowledge has disastrous consequences for understanding the Bible as an inspired religious text.

In the face of the magnificence of the universe, Scripture insists that we bow in wonder before its Creator. Our increased knowledge of the world today, from the complexity inside an atom to the vastness of the universe, should increase our awe at the God who brought it into being and sustains it in existence. The most foundational truth of Christian faith is that God is the one eternal Creator and all others in existence are creatures. The totality of what exists, expressed by the phrase "heaven and earth," depends on the Creator who gives it being.

St. Hilary, a fourth-century Doctor of the Church, reflects on this mystery of God and his creation:

> God is infinite, for nothing contains him and he contains all things; he is eternally unconditioned by space, for he is illimitable; eternally anterior to time, for time is his creation. Let imagination range to what you may suppose is God's utmost limit, and you will find him present there; strain as you will there is always a further horizon toward which to strain. Infinity is his property, just as the power of making such effort is yours. Words will fail you, but his being will not be circumscribed. (Hilary of Poitiers, *On the Trinity* II, 6)

Heaven and earth did not exist eternally with God. Rather, God created all things by the power of his word out of nothing. Thus, the inherent meaning of the universe lies beyond its own limits and is found in God, who causes it, sustains it, and loves it.

Isaiah's prophecy declares that God alone reigns supreme as the just and loving sovereign of the universe. Even the stars and planets, whose movements the Babylonians believed shaped human destinies on earth, are creatures of God (Isa 40:26). Because there is one ultimate source of all things, the Creator and Lord, God's people can entrust their future to him. Although "his understanding is unsearchable," they can depend on God's incomparable power and wisdom with single-minded trust.

Psalm 8 is a hymn of praise, celebrating God as the Creator in awe and wonder. Since God's majesty is evident in all creation, our rightful response is to cry out in praise and worship. Although the vastness of the night sky and God's arrangement of the heavenly bodies can lead us to feel insignificant, God has given human beings a share in God's royal rule over the cosmos. "Crowned with glory and honor," we earthly mortals have been appointed to represent God's reign to other creatures. We have been endowed with tremendous dignity and remarkable responsibility in regard to the other creatures of the world.

Reflection and Discussion

- If I didn't have access to God's revelation in Scripture, what would I know about God from the world around us? Where in creation do I find myself especially aware of the power and wisdom of God?

- Why is it destructive to the credibility of Christian witness for believers to oppose scientific hypotheses about the origins of the universe and the evolution of species? How can I reconcile the verified theories of science with my trust in divine revelation?

- Many writers and poets have written poignantly about people feeling lost, lonely, and overwhelmed with the vastness of the universe. In what ways might the doctrine of creation help me to feel more at home in the world?

Prayer

Sovereign Lord, when I look at the vastness and beauty of your creation, I marvel at your wisdom and power. As a steward of your creation, give me a desire to care for your creatures and embody your reign in the world.

Are not all angels spirits in the divine service, sent to serve for the sake of those who are to inherit salvation?
HEBREWS 1:14

Of All Things Visible and Invisible

1 TIMOTHY 4:4–5 *4For everything created by God is good, and nothing is to be rejected, provided it is received with thanksgiving; 5for it is sanctified by God's word and by prayer.*

HEBREWS 1:10–14 *10And,*
"In the beginning, Lord, you founded the earth,
and the heavens are the work of your hands;
11they will perish, but you remain;
they will all wear out like clothing;
12like a cloak you will roll them up,
and like clothing they will be changed.
But you are the same,
and your years will never end."
13But to which of the angels has he ever said,
"Sit at my right hand
until I make your enemies a footstool for your feet"?
14Are not all angels spirits in the divine service, sent to serve for the sake of those
who are to inherit salvation?

The phrase "of all things visible and invisible" specifies the scope of God's creation, making it clear that God is the first cause of absolutely everything that exists. This specification was needed because of the teachings of second-century Gnosticism, one of the earliest heresies to confront the apostolic faith of the church. Gnostics taught that all spiritual reality is good, while all material reality is evil. The world, they taught, is the battleground for a war between spiritual creation, which is caused by God, and material reality, which is derived from an evil power. According to Gnosticism, human souls are trapped in material bodies and ensnared in a material world. For them, salvation is about escaping the world of matter so that the spiritual self can be free.

Biblical literature opposes this dualistic view of reality and teaches that God is the Creator of heaven and earth, of all things visible and invisible. The material world and spiritual reality are both good and come from the same creative will of God. In fact, both matter and spirit are the goals of God's loving purposes and desire to save the world. As affirmed in Paul's letter to Timothy, "Everything created by God is good, and nothing is to be rejected" (1 Tim 4:4). When we realize that everything around us is a gift from God, we can receive it with thanksgiving. When Christians view the world in this way, everything becomes sacramental, a reflection of its Creator and an occasion of grace.

Christianity today, however, is faced with the opposite problem. For many today, material reality is all that matters. Rampant materialism and consumerism tend to blind people to spiritual reality. The wonders of modern technology and the ease of life it offers convince many that science can solve all mysteries. But revelation teaches us that God is the Creator not only of what we see and understand, but also of what we do not see and can never understand. Beyond all the wondrous discoveries of the modern age, there always remains the Creator whose loving work is not exhausted by the world we see but goes far beyond it, to what we cannot even imagine. We must know that faith in God's revelation is another way of knowing reality, a way that is just as real as the way we come to understand the material world. Practices like prayer and contemplation reveal and reinforce perceptions of the world that include "things visible and invisible."

When we read Scripture, we realize that God has created not only a material world; he has created a cosmos that is infinitely more splendid and diverse than we can envision. The purely spiritual beings whom God has created are called angels. Like human beings, they are relational creatures with minds and wills. This means they can interact with other creatures, think, make choices, and love. But unlike human beings, they have no bodies. Because they are not part of the material world, we can't study them scientifically, not even with microscopes and telescopes. The only way we know of the reality of angels is that God has revealed their existence to us.

It seems that God created the angels before he created material creation. The book of Job says that "all the heavenly beings shouted for joy" when God created the Earth (Job 38:7). They were created for basically the same purpose that we are created: to love and serve God. They are simultaneously turned toward God in worship and turned toward human beings as bearers of God's revelation, providence, and protection.

Reflection and Discussion

- Since Gnostic dualism denied the goodness of all created things and taught that matter, especially the human body, was evil, what might be some lingering Gnosticism within Christian thought today, especially with regard to the body and sexuality?

- How is the belief that the visible, material world does not contain the totality of reality a countercultural challenge to our society today? What are the implications of an understanding of the world that contains both material and spiritual reality?

Prayer

Creator of all, out of your love you have created all creatures, things visible and invisible. You have made human beings a unique combination of spirit and body, incorporating both the visible and invisible realms of creation. Help me to realize the dignity of my being and your loving and eternal care for me.

SUGGESTIONS FOR FACILITATORS, GROUP SESSION 2

1. If there are newcomers who were not present for the first group session, introduce them now.

2. You may want to pray this prayer as a group:
   Sovereign Lord, when we see the vastness and beauty of your creation, we marvel at your wisdom and power. You are the source and cause of all that exists and your eternal power and creative love can be seen in both your visible and invisible creation. Since you have instilled in all people a natural yearning and desire for you, help us to recognize the restless probing of our hearts and show us ways to seek out the confused hearts of others who are searching for you. Give us a heartfelt love for you and a genuine desire to do your will in all things.

3. Ask one or both of the following questions:
   - What was your biggest challenge in Bible study over this past week?
   - What did you learn about yourself this week?

4. Discuss lessons 1 through 6 together. Assuming that group members have read the Scripture and commentary during the week, there is no need to read it aloud. As you review each lesson, you might want to briefly summarize the Scripture passages of each lesson and ask the group what stands out most clearly from the commentary.

5. Choose one or more of the questions for reflection and discussion from each lesson to talk over as a group. You may want to ask group members which question was most challenging or helpful to them as you review each lesson.

6. Keep the discussion moving, but don't rush it in order to complete more questions. Allow time for the questions that provoke the best discussion.

7. Instruct group members to complete lessons 7 through 12 on their own during the six days before the next group meeting. They should write out their own answers to the questions as preparation for next week's group discussion.

8. Conclude by praying aloud together the prayer at the end of lesson 6 or any other prayer you choose.

LESSON 7 SESSION 3

God is faithful; by him you were called into the fellowship of his Son, Jesus Christ our Lord. 1 CORINTHIANS 1:9

One Lord Jesus Christ

MATTHEW 16:13–17 13*Now when Jesus came into the district of Caesarea*
Philippi, he asked his disciples, "Who do people say that the Son of Man is?"
14*And they said, "Some say John the Baptist, but others Elijah, and still others*
Jeremiah or one of the prophets." 15*He said to them, "But who do you say that I*
am?" 16*Simon Peter answered, "You are the Messiah, the Son of the living God."*
17*And Jesus answered him, "Blessed are you, Simon son of Jonah! For flesh and*
blood has not revealed this to you, but my Father in heaven."

1 CORINTHIANS 1:1–9 1*Paul, called to be an apostle of Christ Jesus by the will*
of God, and our brother Sosthenes,

2*To the church of God that is in Corinth, to those who are sanctified in Christ*
Jesus, called to be saints, together with all those who in every place call on the name
of our Lord Jesus Christ, both their Lord and ours:

3*Grace to you and peace from God our Father and the Lord Jesus Christ.*

4*I give thanks to my God always for you because of the grace of God that has*
been given you in Christ Jesus, 5*for in every way you have been enriched in him,*
*in speech and knowledge of every kind—*6*just as the testimony of Christ has been*
*strengthened among you—*7*so that you are not lacking in any spiritual gift as*
you wait for the revealing of our Lord Jesus Christ. 8*He will also strengthen you*
to the end, so that you may be blameless on the day of our Lord Jesus Christ.
9*God is faithful; by him you were called into the fellowship of his Son, Jesus Christ*
our Lord.

Among the many titles given to Jesus in the New Testament, "Christ/Messiah," "Son of God," and "Lord" are supreme among all others. Each is a title of faith, revealed by God to express the truth about who Jesus is. By calling on Jesus with each of these titles, we are reaffirming the most ancient and basic of all Christian beliefs. No single title of Jesus can integrate the fullness of his identity, but each title expresses something unique about his multifaceted nature.

When Jesus asked Peter, "Who do you say I am," Peter responded, "You are the Messiah, the Son of the living God" (Matt 16:16). Messiah is a Hebrew word meaning "anointed," referring to one who was ceremonially anointed with oil for a sacred purpose. The word in Greek is *Christos*, translated as "Christ." Prophets, priests, and kings were anointed with the oil of the olive for the offices in which they served. Because their missions were temporary and failed to fulfill God's desires for his kingdom, Israel increasingly anticipated the coming of *the* Anointed One, *the* Messiah, who would fulfill the expectations expressed in Israel's Scriptures. Likewise, the title "Son of God" is rooted in the Old Testament, referring to Israel as God's firstborn son and the kings of David's line as sons of God. While the sonship of Israel and her kings was fraught with neglect, Jesus was a faithful and obedient Son living in intimate relationship with his Father.

Even though Peter was unable at that time to fully understand the nature of Jesus' divine mission as Messiah and Son of God, Jesus stated that Peter's understanding was divinely inspired: "For flesh and blood has not revealed this to you, but my Father in heaven" (Matt 16:17). Peter expresses a belief that is not possible through human insight alone but that can be attained only through God's grace. This climactic statement of faith is then developed throughout the gospel until it can be fully understood in Christ's death and resurrection.

The third of these titles of Jesus, "Lord," is used for God throughout the Scriptures. The personal name of God, YHWH, is translated into Greek as "Lord" (*Kyrios* in Greek) and used in the New Testament for both God and Jesus. It means that Jesus shares in the power and authority of the Lord God. Not only is he the Messiah of Israel, he is exalted to God's right hand by virtue of his resurrection and reigns supreme over all earthly and heavenly creatures.

Paul and other writers invoke the "Lord Jesus Christ," referring to his risen glory and sovereign authority. When the early Christians called upon him in these words, they recognized him as Lord of all, worthy of the same worship and obedience given to God. Calling Jesus "Lord" was a subversive and sometimes even seditious declaration. Ordered to burn incense to the emperor's image and to proclaim him as the lord, many Christians refused and were put to death. When we profess that Jesus is Lord, we declare that our ultimate allegiance is not to any nation or earthly authority. We declare that the Lord of the whole cosmos is our Lord, acknowledging his sovereignty over our hearts and over our lives.

The core of Christian belief is a person, not a set of abstract ideas. Jesus is the center of the church's faith. Paul refers to Christians as those who "call on the name of our Lord Jesus Christ" (1 Cor 1:2). As both Christ and Lord, Jesus reigns in the hearts of believers and over the whole world. This Christian understanding that Jesus is the Christ, the Messiah or anointed one, was gradually revealed during his earthly life. But the revelation that Jesus is the divine Lord came to be understood by his followers only after his resurrection.

The early church understood Jesus as the Christ and Lord at the experiential level before an explanation of his divinity became necessary. When Paul salutes the Corinthians—"grace to you and peace"—he hails them "from God our Father and the Lord Jesus Christ" (1 Cor 1:3). His careful statement anticipates the ongoing efforts of the early church to clarify the relationship of God and Jesus. By appointing the name "God" to the Father and "Lord" to Jesus Christ, he ascribes divinity to both. The more precise relationship between the Father and the Son will be illuminated more elaborately as the creed develops in the church's first few centuries.

Reflection and Discussion

- Why was it so difficult for Jewish Christians to maintain the faith of their Israelite ancestors and also proclaim the divinity of Jesus?

- What do I mean when I profess "one Lord Jesus Christ"? What other lords am I denying? What am I risking by declaring Jesus as Lord?

- If Jesus is our Lord, then nothing else is lord over our lives and no one is lord over another. In what ways do I experience this paradox of subservience and freedom in Jesus Christ?

- How willing am I to entrust my security, my possessions, and my future to Jesus Christ? What can I do today to demonstrate that Jesus is truly Lord in my life?

Prayer

Lord Jesus Christ, I believe that you are the chosen one of God and that you reign over all creation. Extend your reign over all parts of my life so that my words and actions testify that you are Lord.

"I glorified you on earth by finishing the work that you gave me to do. So now, Father, glorify me in your own presence with the glory that I had in your presence before the world existed." JOHN 17:4–5

The Only Begotten Son of God

JOHN 3:16–21 16*"For God so loved the world that he gave his only Son, so that
everyone who believes in him may not perish but may have eternal life.*
17*"Indeed, God did not send the Son into the world to condemn the world, but in
order that the world might be saved through him.* 18*Those who believe in him are not
condemned; but those who do not believe are condemned already, because they have
not believed in the name of the only Son of God.* 19*And this is the judgment, that the
light has come into the world, and people loved darkness rather than light because
their deeds were evil.* 20*For all who do evil hate the light and do not come to the light,
so that their deeds may not be exposed.* 21*But those who do what is true come to the
light, so that it may be clearly seen that their deeds have been done in God."*

JOHN 17:1–5 1*After Jesus had spoken these words, he looked up to heaven and
said, "Father, the hour has come; glorify your Son so that the Son may glorify you,*
2*since you have given him authority over all people, to give eternal life to all whom
you have given him.* 3*And this is eternal life, that they may know you, the only true
God, and Jesus Christ whom you have sent.* 4*I glorified you on earth by finishing
the work that you gave me to do.* 5*So now, Father, glorify me in your own presence
with the glory that I had in your presence before the world existed.*

The gospels designate Jesus as the Son of God on many occasions, but his unique filial relationship with the Father is particularly emphasized at his baptism and transfiguration, in which a voice from heaven declared of him, "This is my Son, the Beloved" (Matt 3:17; 17:5). Paul, too, speaks of Jesus as God's "own Son," whom he did not withhold from death (Rom 8:32).

John's gospel specifies that Jesus is "the only Son" of God (3:16, 18). The Greek word translated here as "only" is *monogenes*, which literally means "only begotten." John states that God "gave" his only Son out of love for the world, and that God "sent" his Son so that the world might be saved through him. God's giving and sending his only begotten Son implies the Son's existence prior to his coming into the world. The Son is the source of "eternal life," which only God can give. He was sent for the "salvation" of all who believe in him, an achievement that only God could accomplish.

This description of God's Son as "only begotten" implies that the Son is not something made by the Father as part of creation. God's begetting the Son is not physical but spiritual, a sharing by the Father out of himself. The Son shares in the Father's own existence; he is co-equal, inseparable, and united with the Father in one absolute divine essence and being. And since the Father is eternal, the Son is eternally begotten of his Father.

Throughout his gospel, John's narrative elaborates on this eternal unity between the Father and the Son. In the final discourse of Jesus, spoken on the night before his death, Jesus turns from addressing his disciples and lifts his eyes in prayer to his Father (17:1). This climactic prayer of the Son to the Father extends from the time before the world existed, when he was in the Father's presence, to the complete accomplishment of his earthly ministry. "The hour has come" for the climax of his life. Jesus asks the Father to "glorify" the Son: "Glorify me in your own presence with the glory that I had in your presence before the world existed" (17:5). Jesus had glorified the Father, externally manifesting God's deep and hidden nature, through his wondrous teachings and signs, but the full revelation of God's nature would occur as Jesus offers his life on the cross. The glorification of the Son is the manifestation of God's love to the whole world. The Son's deepest nature is his glory as the eternal Word of God, the glory he had in his Father's presence before his mission in our human history and even before creation itself.

As the revealing ministry of Jesus is ending and he is about to return to the Father, Jesus does not want to return to the Father alone. He wants to take us with him. The purpose of his mission in the world is to give us "eternal life." The unique value of this life is not just the fact that it lasts forever. More importantly, it is a new quality of life for the believer. Eternal life is God's own life, a life that he wants us to share because he loves us so much. Jesus describes this life as "knowing" the Father and the Son. This knowing is a personal, experiential union with God, an experience that is entered through the gift of faith when we surrender to God's incomparable love.

Various heresies in the early church taught that Jesus was not fully God. They taught that he was a uniquely made creature or that he was adopted as God's Son at some moment in time. But orthodox Christian belief holds that God is fully present in Jesus in a fullness not realized in any other person. St. Athanasius and other Fathers of the church kept the focus of early Christian debate on the redemptive work of Christ. Jesus is God's only Son through whom God is reconciling the world to himself. In him we experience forgiveness and share in God's own life. Another who is merely human cannot elevate us to the level of God, but human salvation is achieved through God entering our humanity in Christ. Through the humanity of his Son, God made it possible for all people to share in the divine life.

Reflection and Discussion

- What fuller understanding of John 3:16 have I been given? What does the gospel mean when it says that God "gave" and "sent" his "only begotten Son"?

- In what ways have I experienced "eternal life"? How can I surrender myself more fully to God's love in order to experience a more personal union with God?

Prayer

Eternal Son of God, you have revealed the true nature and love of God to us through your life, death, and resurrection. Help me to experience a fuller understanding of God and union with him as I long to share eternal life more deeply and completely.

LESSON 9 SESSION 3

And the Word became flesh and lived among us, and we have seen his glory, the glory as of a father's only son, full of grace and truth. JOHN 1:14

Consubstantial with the Father

JOHN 1:1–5, 10–14, 16–18 *[1]In the beginning was the Word, and the Word was with God, and the Word was God. [2]He was in the beginning with God. [3]All things came into being through him, and without him not one thing came into being. What has come into being [4]in him was life, and the life was the light of all people. [5]The light shines in the darkness, and the darkness did not overcome it.*

[10]He was in the world, and the world came into being through him; yet the world did not know him. [11]He came to what was his own, and his own people did not accept him. [12]But to all who received him, who believed in his name, he gave power to become children of God, [13]who were born, not of blood or of the will of the flesh or of the will of man, but of God.

[14]And the Word became flesh and lived among us, and we have seen his glory, the glory as of a father's only son, full of grace and truth… [16]From his fullness we have all received, grace upon grace. [17]The law indeed was given through Moses; grace and truth came through Jesus Christ. [18]No one has ever seen God. It is God the only Son, who is close to the Father's heart, who has made him known.

"The Word" is God's self-expression. Just as a human word is, in a sense, the extension of a person into their environment, so the divine Word is God's reaching out, sharing his divine being with creation. A human word reveals hidden thoughts; the divine Word reveals the hidden nature of God, demonstrating that God is compassionate, loving, and forgiving.

Since the Word existed "in the beginning," either the Word was with God or the Word was God. John's gospel affirms both (verse 1). The text suggests a distinction between the Word and God, but not a separation. Everything came into being through the Word. God's Word began to be known first through creation, then through the Torah and prophets of Israel, and finally through Jesus Christ. As God's self-expression, "the Word" encompasses the preexistence of the Son of God, his entire ministry in the world, and his eternal existence with the Father.

In Jesus Christ, "the Word became flesh" (verse 14). The eternal Word has been born into frail humanity. In the Word made flesh, God has chosen to be with his people in a more personal way than ever before. John shows that the incarnation is on a scale with the creation of the world. In this new creation, the incarnate Word gives to humankind the power to become children of God, to be reborn, not of natural descent or human initiative, but of God (verse 13). This is the ultimate reason why the Word became flesh: so that we might be raised up to share intimately in God's life.

In order to preserve the full testimony of Scripture regarding the relationship of the Father and the Son, the Council of Nicaea used the Greek term *homoousios,* translated as "consubstantial" or "one in being." Whatever is the essence of that which constitutes deity, it is the same for the Father and for the Son. Though they are distinct as persons, God the Father and God the Son are the same being. They are of the same essence; that is, truly the same God.

To emphasize the divinity of Jesus the Son and his unity with the Father, the creed insists that he is "God from God, Light from Light, true God from true God." The image of light is one of the most influential metaphors for God in the Bible because, of all material things, light comes closest to the spiritual. The psalms consistently associate light with God: "The Lord is my light" (Ps 27:1) and "In your light we see light" (Ps 36:9). The shining out of God's light into the world's darkness is a frequent biblical expression for God's self-manifestation among his creation (Isa 2:5; 9:2; 60:1–3). John's gospel declares that "the Word" is "the light of all people"; he is the light that shines in the darkness, the light that the darkness cannot overcome (verses 4–5). Through the divine light of the Son of God, people are able to see the world correctly, even though it is swallowed in darkness. Through the metaphor of light, the Scriptures progressively clarify that God is the source of light and the Son is the light's luminescence. The Word is the light that shines out of the light: Light from Light, true God from true God.

This consubstantial unity of the Father and the Son was taught by St. Athanasius in the fourth century. Insisting that "the whole being of the Son is proper to the Father's essence," he taught that the Son is "from the Father" as is "radiance from light," "the stream from the fountain," and "the word from the thought" (Athanasius, *Discourse Three Against the Arians*, 23:3). The Son comes from the Father yet is also of the same essence as the Father, just as the rays of light come from the light yet they are the same substance. Similarly, the stream of water comes from its flowing source, yet both the fountain and the stream are the same essence of flowing water. Likewise, the word is a manifestation of the thought, yet the thought and the word are one in being. With this teaching, Athanasius follows the full witness of John's gospel, beginning in the prologue and continuing through Jesus' enigmatic question, "Do you not believe that I am in the Father and the Father is in me?" (14:10). The light and its rays, the fountain and its stream, the thought and its word: their names and appearances are different, yet they are "consubstantial" with each other. The former is, so to speak, father of the latter. The latter is begotten of the former. So, too, the Father and the Son are consubstantial, yet the Son is begotten of the Father.

Reflection and Discussion

- In what ways does the metaphor of light help me to comprehend something of the relationship between the Father and the Son?

- John makes it clear that the Word did not become manifest in the world merely as an apparition, but truly "became flesh and lived among us." What difference does this divine "enfleshment" mean for my life?

- Seeing the wounds in the hands and side of the risen Jesus, the doubts of Thomas gave way to a living faith as he uttered these climactic words: "My Lord and my God!" (20:28). In what ways can the emerging faith of Thomas be a model for those who doubt and struggle with faith?

- What are the dark places of my mind and heart? What do I need to remove or uncover in order to let the light of Christ fill my life today?

Prayer

Word of God, you shine in the world and bring divine radiance to all creation. Cast out the darkness of ignorance and falsehood, and show the world the truth, goodness, and love of God. Open my heart to the "grace upon grace" that you desire for me to experience in your light.

He is the image of the invisible God, the firstborn of all creation; for in him all things in heaven and on earth were created, things visible and invisible. COLOSSIANS 1:15–16

Through Him All Things Were Made

1 CORINTHIANS 8:4–6 4*Hence, as to the eating of food offered to idols, we know*
that "no idol in the world really exists," and that "there is no God but one." 5*Indeed,*
even though there may be so-called gods in heaven or on earth—as in fact there are
*many gods and many lords—*6*yet for us there is one God, the Father, from whom*
are all things and for whom we exist, and one Lord, Jesus Christ, through whom
are all things and through whom we exist.

COLOSSIANS 1:15–20 15*He is the image of the invisible God, the firstborn of all*
creation; 16*for in him all things in heaven and on earth were created, things visible*
and invisible, whether thrones or dominions or rulers or powers—all things have
been created through him and for him. 17*He himself is before all things, and in him*
all things hold together. 18*He is the head of the body, the church; he is the begin-*
ning, the firstborn from the dead, so that he might come to have first place in every-
thing. 19*For in him all the fullness of God was pleased to dwell,* 20*and through him*
God was pleased to reconcile to himself all things, whether on earth or in heaven,
by making peace through the blood of his cross.

HEBREWS 1:1–3 1*Long ago God spoke to our ancestors in many and various*
ways by the prophets, 2*but in these last days he has spoken to us by a Son, whom*
he appointed heir of all things, through whom he also created the worlds. 3*He is the*

reflection of God's glory and the exact imprint of God's very being, and he sustains all things by his powerful word.

In the context of Paul's pastoral advice about the common practice of eating food offered to idols, Paul vividly proclaims the belief of the early Christians. Although there are many "so-called gods," the deities of the Greco-Roman pantheon, and many so-called lords, including figures venerated in the eastern mystery cults, Christians believe in "one God, the Father" and "one Lord, Jesus Christ" (1 Cor 8:6). God is the one from whom all things came into being and for whom believers live. Jesus Christ is the Lord who mediates God's creative and redemptive powers so that God's will is made real in the world. Through him all things came into being, and through him believers live. In relationship to the one God and one Lord, Christians find a new identity and new way of life.

Paul continues this line of thought in his great hymn to Christ's supremacy. By calling Christ "the image [*eikon*, in Greek] of the invisible God" (Col 1:15), he means that Christ shares in the nature of God and visibly reveals and manifests God in human form. As the icon of God, Jesus Christ stands supreme over created reality as "the firstborn [*prototokos*, in Greek] of all creation." Although some heretical teachers took this designation of Christ in a temporal sense to suggest that he was part of God's creation, Paul is proclaiming Christ's primacy over creation. Paul emphatically declares that "all things" were created in Christ: those "in heaven and on earth," both "visible and invisible," even the most powerful forces of the spiritual world (Col 1:16).

Yet, not only were all things created "through" Christ, but all were created "for" him. In other words, Christ is both the divine agent of creation and the final goal of creation. As the one through whom and for whom God made the world, he is not just one of the many spiritual powers. He is the preexisting Lord over all creation, and all powers are subject to the primacy of Christ. All things "hold together" in him as their source of coherence, stability, and purpose (Col 1:17). Nothing in the universe exists for its own sake. Everything from the smallest particle to the biggest star, from the bottom of the oceans to the top of the mountains, exists for Christ.

As Lord of creation, Christ is also Lord of his church and gives the church its universal mission (Col 1:18). His resurrection animates and enlivens the church. Because "the fullness of God" dwells in him, he is the divine agent not only of God's creating will but also of God's redeeming will. Through Christ, God reconciled absolutely everything in the universe to himself, extending peace and wholeness to creation through Christ's sacrificial death on the cross.

The writer of Hebrews begins his letter by recalling how God spoke his word in the past through the ancestors of Israel, but how he has now spoken his final and climactic word through his Son. This divine Son is not only the one through whom God created the world in the beginning, but also "the heir of all things" at the end (Heb 1:1–2). Everything that God had previously done in the world was preparatory, pointing to its goal and ultimate meaning in Christ. The Son is "the reflection of God's glory," the radiant light that comes from the source of light, and he is "the exact imprint of God's very being," the impress of the divine essence (Heb 1:3). Both of these descriptions insist that the Son participates in the very being of God. Without denying the distinction between the Father and the Son, the author insists that the Son is of the same order of existence as God.

Each of these three writings expresses the early faith of the church that all things are from God the Father and all things are equally through God the Son. Through God's revelation in creation and redemption, we are drawn into the mystery of God's own life. We realize that the incarnation of the Son in the world has made explicit the presence of the Son that was always implicit in creation itself. The coming of the Son in the flesh is the full manifestation in the world of the divine Word, the image and exact imprint of the unseen God.

Reflection and Discussion

- In what ways do each of the above three letters reinforce and elaborate John's message that "all things came into being through him, and without him not one thing came into being" (John 1:3)?

- What are some of the implications of the teaching in these letters that all things exist through and for Jesus, the Son of God?

- How does understanding that Jesus Christ is the "icon" of the invisible God, the "reflection of the Father's glory," help me to better appreciate his divinity in relationship to the Father?

- Since Christ is the source and goal of my life, how can I live more consciously and fully through him, with him, and in him?

Prayer

Lord Jesus Christ, through you I have come into being, through you I am redeemed from sin and death, and through you I am called to eternal life. Because I have been created for you, may my life give you glory through all that I say and do.

Though he was in the form of God, [Jesus Christ] did not regard equality with God as something to be exploited, but emptied himself, taking the form of a slave, being born in human likeness. PHILIPPIANS 2:6–7

For Our Salvation He Came Down from Heaven

PHILIPPIANS 2:5–11 5 *Let the same mind be in you that was in Christ Jesus,*
6 *who, though he was in the form of God,*
did not regard equality with God
as something to be exploited,
7 *but emptied himself,*
taking the form of a slave,
being born in human likeness.
And being found in human form,
8 *he humbled himself*
and became obedient to the point of death—
even death on a cross.

9 *Therefore God also highly exalted him*
and gave him the name
that is above every name,
10 *so that at the name of Jesus*
every knee should bend,
in heaven and on earth and under the earth,

> 11 *and every tongue should confess*
> *that Jesus Christ is Lord,*
> *to the glory of God the Father.*

If salvation were simply a matter of fixing the political and social structures of society, then Jesus need be no more than a moral and charismatic leader. Or if salvation were only about changing mistaken ideas and beliefs, then Jesus need be no more than a great teacher. But the New Testament tells us that salvation is a matter of liberation from all the cosmic forces that keeps creation enslaved and of reconciling the world to God. Because salvation is God's cosmic victory on behalf of the world and humanity, then Jesus the Savior must be not only fully human but also fully divine.

To proclaim that the Son of God "came down from heaven" means that he "descended" from the realm of God and entered fully into our world. Paul describes this descent as a change in status. Though he participated in the very essence of God, Jesus Christ did not exploit his divine status, using his divinity for his own self-assertion or glory. Rather, he emptied himself and humbled himself, entering fully into the human condition. He renounced every advantage or privilege that might have accrued to him, becoming subservient to all the forces and powers that determine human life. He subjected himself to suffering and death, even execution on a cross, as an opportunity for unreserved self-sacrifice.

Jesus taking the form of a slave does not mean that he exchanged the nature of God for the nature of a slave. Rather, he displayed the nature of God in and through the nature of a slave. He displayed the nature of God in the act of humble service and sacrifice. From the manger to the tomb, the life of God-with-us was marked by lowliness.

Christ's descent into the lowest depth, through his humiliating crucifixion, was reversed as God exalted him to the highest place of authority and honor. Dishonored and disgraced in his humanity, God divinely vindicated Jesus in that same humanity. God gave him the name that is above every other name. The God who declared, "To me every knee shall bow, every tongue shall swear" (Isa 45:23), now exalts Jesus Christ "so that at the name of Jesus every knee should bend" throughout creation. The God who declared, "I am the

Lord, that is my name; my glory I give to no other" (Isa 42:8), now bestows that name upon Jesus and urges all creation to confess that "Jesus Christ is Lord." When divine titles and honors are given to the humiliated and exalted Christ, the glory of God the Father is not diminished but enhanced. When the Son is honored, the Father is glorified; for no higher honors can be conferred upon the Son than the Father himself has conferred.

Paul urges his readers, "Let the same mind be in you that was in Christ Jesus" (verse 5). The lesson for the Christians of Philippi is clear: as Christ set aside his own interests for the sake of others, so should they. When we have taken on the humility and the servant attitude of Christ, we are able to imitate him in our relationships with one another. The crucified Lord is the model of sacrificial service of others. As Jesus himself said, "All who humble themselves will be exalted" (Matt 23:12). His saving act on the cross empowers us to live transformed lives, as servants of one another and as people destined for eternal life with him.

The creed describes the Son of God: first in relationship with the Father and then in relationship with humanity, beginning with his incarnation. Yet, this order of the creed is not the order of the discovery of these truths of faith in the church. The Christian community first experienced the humanity of Jesus and then began to appreciate his divinity and his unity with the Father. Through experiencing the risen Christ, they began to understand the divine power and authority of the Messiah who shared so deeply in their humanity. In experiencing his continuing personal and transcendent presence, they came to believe in Jesus' unique relationship with God.

Reflection and Discussion

- Why is it so critically important for salvation that Jesus be both God and human?

- As this hymn was sung at Christian baptisms in which one went under the water to die with Christ and came out of the water to rise with him, in what way does the hymn describe the transforming power of baptism?

- Since Paul urges us to take on the mind of Christ and to live in him, how can I more fully take on the humility and the servant attitude of Christ and imitate him in my relationships with others?

- Paul ended his hymn with the earliest and quintessential creed of the church: "Jesus Christ is Lord." What does it mean to me to profess that Jesus is the Lord?

Prayer

Lord Jesus Christ, help me to imitate your humility, share in your suffering, and serve others with obedience and sacrificial love. Thank you for taking on my humanity and for raising me up to share in your divinity.

Mary said to the angel, "How can this be, since I am a virgin?" The angel said to her, "The Holy Spirit will come upon you, and the power of the Most High will overshadow you." LUKE 1:34–35

Incarnate of the Virgin Mary

MATTHEW 1:18–25 [18]*Now the birth of Jesus the Messiah took place in this way.*
When his mother Mary had been engaged to Joseph, but before they lived together,
she was found to be with child from the Holy Spirit. [19]*Her husband Joseph, being a*
righteous man and unwilling to expose her to public disgrace, planned to dismiss her
quietly. [20]*But just when he had resolved to do this, an angel of the Lord appeared to*
him in a dream and said, "Joseph, son of David, do not be afraid to take Mary as
your wife, for the child conceived in her is from the Holy Spirit. [21]*She will bear a son,*
and you are to name him Jesus, for he will save his people from their sins." [22]*All this*
took place to fulfill what had been spoken by the Lord through the prophet:

> [23]*"Look, the virgin shall conceive and bear a son,*
> *and they shall name him Emmanuel,"*

which means, "God is with us." [24]*When Joseph awoke from sleep, he did as the*
angel of the Lord commanded him; he took her as his wife, [25]*but had no marital*
relations with her until she had borne a son; and he named him Jesus.

LUKE 1:26–38 [26]*In the sixth month the angel Gabriel was sent by God to a town*
in Galilee called Nazareth, [27]*to a virgin engaged to a man whose name was Joseph,*
of the house of David. The virgin's name was Mary. [28]*And he came to her and said,*
"Greetings, favored one! The Lord is with you." [29]*But she was much perplexed by*
his words and pondered what sort of greeting this might be. [30]*The angel said to her,*
"Do not be afraid, Mary, for you have found favor with God. [31]*And now, you will*
conceive in your womb and bear a son, and you will name him Jesus. [32]*He will be*

great, and will be called the Son of the Most High, and the Lord God will give to him the throne of his ancestor David. [33]He will reign over the house of Jacob forever, and of his kingdom there will be no end." [34]Mary said to the angel, "How can this be, since I am a virgin?" [35]The angel said to her, "The Holy Spirit will come upon you, and the power of the Most High will overshadow you; therefore the child to be born will be holy; he will be called Son of God. [36]And now, your relative Elizabeth in her old age has also conceived a son; and this is the sixth month for her who was said to be barren. [37]For nothing will be impossible with God." [38]Then Mary said, "Here am I, the servant of the Lord; let it be with me according to your word." Then the angel departed from her.

The Apostles' Creed states that Jesus Christ was "conceived by the Holy Spirit, born of the Virgin Mary." The agency of the incarnation is equally the Spirit, who is designated as Holy, and Mary, who is designated as Virgin. The Nicene Creed does not distinguish between conception and birth but affirms the instrumentality of both the Holy Spirit and the Virgin Mary in the Son of God being made flesh and becoming human. Each statement affirms both the work of God in the incarnation of Christ and his real participation in the human condition.

The language of each creed comes from the annunciation accounts of both Matthew and Luke. Matthew narrates the event from Joseph's point of view and states that Mary is found to be pregnant after her betrothal to Joseph but before they began living together. Unwilling to expose Mary to the public disgrace of adultery, he had decided to divorce her quietly when an angel told Joseph not to fear to take Mary as his wife, "for the child conceived in her is from the Holy Spirit" (Matt 1:20). Matthew reinforces this account by citing a passage from Isaiah 7:14 in the Septuagint version, a Greek translation of Scripture, read among the Jewish people before the Christian era: "The virgin shall conceive and bear a son, and they shall name him Emmanuel."

Luke immediately identifies Mary as a virgin (Luke 1:27). His narrative, told from the perspective of Mary, describes the appearance of an angel, announcing to Mary that she will conceive in her womb and bear a son (Luke 1:31). When Mary objects because she has not had sexual relations, the angel said to her, "The Holy Spirit will come upon you, and the power of the Most High will overshadow you; therefore the child to be born will be holy; he will be called Son of God" (Luke 1:35).

The ancient Christian writers understood that these evangelists taught that the conception of Jesus was a miraculous intervention of the Holy Spirit in the young life of the Virgin Mary. St. Augustine, in his Christmas homily, captures some of the wonder of the incarnation: "My brethren, what miracles! What prodigies! The laws of nature are changed in the case of man. God is born. A virgin becomes pregnant with man. The Word of God marries the woman who knows no man. She is now at the same time both mother and virgin. She becomes a mother, yet she remains a virgin" (Augustine, Sermo 13 *de Tempore*).

Yet, it is not the biology of the conception that preoccupied the early Christians. Instead, what was important to them was that the incarnation of God's Son came about through both divine and human agency. The Spirit of God that swept over the waters at creation and stirred the prophets to speak is now active in the life of Mary as the Son of God "came down from heaven." The conception of Jesus and his birth from the womb of Mary indicate that he shares fully in the human condition within the body and the world of a young Jewish woman from Nazareth in Galilee. This Jesus, who will save his people from their sins, is both Son of God and Son of Mary.

The theme of the barren woman who conceives runs throughout the Hebrew Scriptures. Sarah, Rebecca, Rachel, Hannah, and others in the Old Testament, who conceive after many years of barrenness, benefit from a divine intervention to make them fertile. Often in advanced age, they bring forth a child as a demonstration of God's covenant fidelity to his people. This theme continues in the New Testament as the aged Elizabeth conceives and gives birth to John, the forerunner of Jesus. Mary is the culmination of this biblical theme of the barren woman who conceives by divine intervention, just as Jesus is the culmination of Israel's hopes and the completion of God's covenant fidelity. Now the barren one par excellence, the Virgin Mary, conceives by the intervention of the Holy Spirit, an action unlike anything ever before in salvation history. The virginity of Mary highlights the radical newness of God's action. God's intervention was not in response to her yearning for a child, nor was it the result of anything she could have anticipated. God was doing an extraordinarily new thing in response to the watchful longing of his people.

Reflection and Discussion

- What are some of the important theological insights offered by the annunciation accounts of Matthew and Luke?

- In what way do the creeds affirm that Jesus is truly divine by his very nature in opposition to heretical thinkers who proposed that Jesus was only human and that God later adopted him as his Son, at either his baptism or his resurrection?

- How can I trust God more completely, as Mary trusted? How can I open my life to God's presence and let Christ be manifested in the world through me?

Prayer

Most High God, you responded to the watchful longing of your people with the gift of your faithfulness. Give me the desire to respond to you like Mary, most blessed among women. Let your divine will be done in me according to your word.

SUGGESTIONS FOR FACILITATORS, GROUP SESSION 3

1. Welcome group members and ask if anyone has any announcements to make.

2. You may want to pray this prayer as a group:
   Eternal Son of God, Lord Jesus Christ, through you we have come into being, through you we are redeemed from sin and death, and through you we are called to eternal life. Because we are created through you and for you, may the words and actions of our lives give you glory and testify to your faithful love. Thank you for taking on our humanity and for raising us up to share in your divinity. Like Mary, most blessed among women, let your divine will be done in us according to your word.

3. Ask one or both of the following questions:
   - Which message of Scripture this week speaks most powerfully to you?
   - What is the most important lesson you learned through your study this week?

4. Discuss lessons 7 through 12. Choose one or more of the questions for reflection and discussion from each lesson to discuss as a group. You may want to ask group members which question was most challenging or helpful to them as you review each lesson.

5. Remember that there are no definitive answers for these discussion questions. The insights of group members will add to the understanding of all. None of these questions requires an expert.

6. After talking about each lesson, instruct group members to complete lessons 13 through 18 on their own during the six days before the next group meeting. They should write out their own answers to the questions as preparation for next week's group discussion.

7. Ask the group if anyone is having any particular problems with the Bible study during the week. You may want to share advice and encouragement within the group.

8. Conclude by praying aloud together the prayer at the end of one of the lessons discussed. You may add to the prayer based on the sharing that has occurred in the group.

**He himself bore our sins in his body on the cross,
so that, free from sins, we might live for righteousness;
by his wounds you have been healed.** 1 PETER 2:24

Crucified Under Pontius Pilate

MARK 15:12–20 *[12]Pilate spoke to them again, "Then what do you wish me to do with the man you call the King of the Jews?" [13]They shouted back, "Crucify him!" [14]Pilate asked them, "Why, what evil has he done?" But they shouted all the more, "Crucify him!" [15]So Pilate, wishing to satisfy the crowd, released Barabbas for them; and after flogging Jesus, he handed him over to be crucified.*

[16]Then the soldiers led him into the courtyard of the palace (that is, the governor's headquarters); and they called together the whole cohort. [17]And they clothed him in a purple cloak; and after twisting some thorns into a crown, they put it on him. [18]And they began saluting him, "Hail, King of the Jews!" [19]They struck his head with a reed, spat upon him, and knelt down in homage to him. [20]After mocking him, they stripped him of the purple cloak and put his own clothes on him. Then they led him out to crucify him.

1 PETER 2:21–25 *[21]For to this you have been called, because Christ also suffered for you, leaving you an example, so that you should follow in his steps.*

[22]"He committed no sin,
and no deceit was found in his mouth."

[23]When he was abused, he did not return abuse; when he suffered, he did not threaten; but he entrusted himself to the one who judges justly. [24]He himself bore our sins in his body on the cross, so that, free from sins, we might live for righteousness; by his wounds you have been healed. [25]For you were going astray like sheep, but now you have returned to the shepherd and guardian of your souls.

In order to emphasize the human, historical character of Christ's life, the creed highlights his wondrous birth and his torturous death, the manger and the cross. Both the Incarnation and the Redemption stress the true humanity of Jesus in contradiction to the Gnostic teachers within early Christianity who taught that Christ was a spiritual being who only appeared to have a physical body. Mary and Pontius Pilate, the only two human beings mentioned in the creed besides Jesus, ground the birth and death of Jesus in human history and represent two opposite human responses to him.

"Crucified under Pontius Pilate" focuses our attention on the means of Jesus' execution and its political sponsor. This article of the creed leaves out the denial, betrayal, and abandonment of Jesus by his disciples, as well as the complicity of the religious leaders of Jerusalem, so richly narrated in the passion accounts of the four gospels. By passing directly from the birth to the death of Jesus, the creed emphasizes only those elements of his life that demonstrate his true humanity: his real conception and birth from a woman as well as his genuine suffering and death on the cross.

The manner of our salvation through Jesus Christ is the great paradox of Christianity. According to human wisdom, it seems absurd that the Lord of creation should enter human history as an infant, born in an obscure place to impoverished parents. But that the incarnate Lord should be put to death as a criminal, through the cruelest and most shameful form of execution imaginable, seems to be the utmost in foolishness. Yet, here is displayed the paradox of divine strength in human weakness, divine riches in human poverty, and divine wisdom in human foolishness.

The New Testament gives multiple reasons for the crucifixion of Jesus. Paul explains that "Christ died for our sins" (1 Cor 15:3), that his death is "a sacrifice of atonement by his blood" (Rom 3:25), and that "Christ loved us and gave himself up for us" (Eph 5:2). Yet, the first letter of Peter refers more to the cross than any other New Testament letter. Peter had learned so much since the early days when he heard the call of Jesus, "Follow me" (Mark 1:17). At the critical moment of Jesus' arrest, Peter "followed him at a distance" (Mark 14:54) and eventually denied him. Still, at a critical time for the early church, Peter exhorts the suffering community of Jesus' disciples to "follow in his steps" (1 Pet 2:21), in the very footprints of their cross-bearing Lord.

In holding up Jesus as our "example" in suffering, Peter uses descriptive phrases from the Suffering Servant song in Isaiah 53. As the fullest embodiment of this model of suffering, Jesus is the innocent sufferer. Though abused and afflicted, he did not retaliate or seek revenge. He was a model of patient endurance, confidently entrusting himself to "the one who judges justly." As the Suffering Servant, Jesus bore the burdens of our sins so that we might live anew as forgiven and healed people.

Reflection and Discussion

- In what ways do the gospels demonstrate that Mary and Pontius Pilate represent two opposite responses to God's work in Jesus?

- In his first letter, Peter says, "By his wounds you have been healed" (1 Pet 2:24). How do I understand the crucifixion of Jesus as the source of my healing?

- In what ways can I use the wounds of my own suffering to become a healer for others?

Prayer

Wounded Healer, I praise you for submitting to the bondage of the cross so that we might be truly free, for suffering so that we might have real joy, for dying so that we might have eternal life. Transform my suffering into a graced encounter with you so that I may experience your healing.

For if while we were enemies, we were reconciled to God through the death of his Son, much more surely, having been reconciled, will we be saved by his life. ROMANS 5:10

Suffered Death and Was Buried

MARK 15:37–46 37 *Then Jesus gave a loud cry and breathed his last.* 38 *And the*
curtain of the temple was torn in two, from top to bottom. 39 *Now when the cen-*
turion, who stood facing him, saw that in this way he breathed his last, he said,
"Truly this man was God's Son!"

40 *There were also women looking on from a distance; among them were Mary*
Magdalene, and Mary the mother of James the younger and of Joses, and Salome.
41 *These used to follow him and provided for him when he was in Galilee; and there*
were many other women who had come up with him to Jerusalem.

42 *When evening had come, and since it was the day of Preparation, that is, the*
day before the sabbath, 43 *Joseph of Arimathea, a respected member of the council,*
who was also himself waiting expectantly for the kingdom of God, went boldly to
Pilate and asked for the body of Jesus. 44 *Then Pilate wondered if he were already*
dead; and summoning the centurion, he asked him whether he had been dead for
some time. 45 *When he learned from the centurion that he was dead, he granted*
the body to Joseph. 46 *Then Joseph bought a linen cloth, and taking down the body,*
wrapped it in the linen cloth, and laid it in a tomb that had been hewn out of the
rock. He then rolled a stone against the door of the tomb.

ROMANS 5:6–11 6 *For while we were still weak, at the right time Christ died for*
the ungodly. 7 *Indeed, rarely will anyone die for a righteous person—though per-*

haps for a good person someone might actually dare to die. [8]*But God proves his love for us in that while we still were sinners Christ died for us.* [9]*Much more surely then, now that we have been justified by his blood, will we be saved through him from the wrath of God.* [10]*For if while we were enemies, we were reconciled to God through the death of his Son, much more surely, having been reconciled, will we be saved by his life.* [11]*But more than that, we even boast in God through our Lord Jesus Christ, through whom we have now received reconciliation.*

Following Jesus' loud cry from the cross and his last breath, Mark's gospel describes two consequences of his death. First, the temple veil was torn from top to bottom, symbolizing the new access to God which Christ's death won for all people. Second, the Roman centurion confessed his faith in Jesus, expressing his identity as the Son of God (Mark 15:38–39). Both of these consequences signify that on the cross Jesus has established a new, inclusive community of disciples. One of these new disciples is the Roman soldier, a Gentile, a man outside the community of Israel. With him also are the women, those faithful disciples who stood with Jesus at his cross when the others fled. The tearing of the temple curtain dramatically underlines what the people at the foot of the cross express: the cross has made access to God available to all, regardless of race, status, or gender. From now on, the way to forgiveness and unity with God is through the cross.

The suffering and death of Christ are purposeful because they accomplish the redemption of the world. Yet, the passion only begins to be comprehensible when we are moved to ponder the inexplicable character of divine love. As Paul wrote, "God proves his love for us in that while we still were sinners Christ died for us" (Rom 5:8). Jesus' whole life was inspired by his desire to embrace his Father's plan of redeeming love. The depth of God's love for sinners is so self-giving and sacrificial that it exhausts the resources of the human mind to contemplate and comprehend such love. In his suffering and death, the humanity of Jesus became the free and perfect instrument of his divine love, which desires the salvation of all humanity.

The ancient tradition remembers that immediately after the death of Jesus, he was buried. The gospel states that Jesus' body was wrapped in a linen cloth and laid in a rock-hewn tomb, over the entrance of which a stone was rolled.

The fact that Jesus was buried and remained in the tomb for some time confirms the physical reality of his death. Traditional Jewish belief held that the souls of the dead went to a place below the earth to await the final resurrection. So, the early Christians believed that Jesus remained in the underworld, experiencing the full condition of human death. This is the final descent of Jesus into the fullness of the human condition.

The Apostles' Creed added the words "he descended into hell" following Jesus' death and burial and before his resurrection from the dead. The shadowy underworld is called *Sheol* in Hebrew, *Hades* in Greek, and *Infernus* in Latin. The English translation "hell" does not refer, in this case, to the eternal state of separation from God but to this lower-world state of waiting. The souls of the just ones wait in this incomplete state, with their souls separated from their bodies, for the glorious day of resurrection.

Yet, the apostolic writers knew that, in his descent to the realm of the dead, Jesus was not only joining the other souls in death but, as universal Savior, he was bringing salvation to righteous souls who died before the crucifixion. As 1 Peter testifies, Jesus proclaimed the gospel to the spirits imprisoned there (1 Pet 3:19; 4:6). The descent into hell signifies the spread of Christ's redemptive work to all people of all times and all places, for all who are saved have been made sharers in the redemption.

Reflection and Discussion

- Paul states that at the name of Jesus, "every knee should bend, in heaven and on earth and under the earth" (Phil 2:10). In what sense is Jesus' death, burial, and descent to the underworld an expression of his complete cosmic victory?

- In his first speech in Acts, Peter quotes Psalm 16 as fulfilled in Jesus: "You will not abandon my soul to Hades, or let your Holy One experience corruption" (Acts 2:27). How does the fact that Jesus experienced death before us and has promised not to abandon us help me to face my own inevitable death?

- The Orthodox icon for the Feast of the Resurrection shows Jesus coming forth from the underworld, bringing Adam and Eve with him. In what ways does this image express the divine will to save all people?

- Peter urged, "Always be ready to make your defense to anyone who demands from you an accounting for the hope that is in you" (1 Pet 3:15). How can I be a witness to the hope that Jesus Christ has given to me?

Prayer

Merciful God, you have proven your love for me by Christ's death for me, a sinner. I believe that I have been reconciled to you by his death, and I know salvation through his risen life. Thank you for the hope you have given me through his sorrowful passion and his glorious resurrection.

If there is no resurrection of the dead, then Christ has not been raised; and if Christ has not been raised, then our proclamation has been in vain and your faith has been in vain. 1 CORINTHIANS 15:13–14

Rose Again on the Third Day

1 CORINTHIANS 15:1–7, 12–20 [1]*Now I would remind you, brothers and sisters,*
of the good news that I proclaimed to you, which you in turn received, in which also
you stand, [2]*through which also you are being saved, if you hold firmly to the mes-*
sage that I proclaimed to you—unless you have come to believe in vain.

[3]*For I handed on to you as of first importance what I in turn had received: that*
Christ died for our sins in accordance with the scriptures, [4]*and that he was buried,*
and that he was raised on the third day in accordance with the scriptures, [5]*and that*
he appeared to Cephas, then to the twelve. [6]*Then he appeared to more than five*
hundred brothers and sisters at one time, most of whom are still alive, though some
have died. [7]*Then he appeared to James, then to all the apostles.*

[12]*Now if Christ is proclaimed as raised from the dead, how can some of you say*
there is no resurrection of the dead? [13]*If there is no resurrection of the dead, then*
Christ has not been raised; [14]*and if Christ has not been raised, then our proclama-*
tion has been in vain and your faith has been in vain. [15]*We are even found to be mis-*
representing God, because we testified of God that he raised Christ—whom he did
not raise if it is true that the dead are not raised. [16]*For if the dead are not raised, then*
Christ has not been raised. [17]*If Christ has not been raised, your faith is futile and*
you are still in your sins. [18]*Then those also who have died in Christ have perished.*
[19]*If for this life only we have hoped in Christ, we are of all people most to be pitied.*

[20]*But in fact Christ has been raised from the dead, the first fruits of those who have died.*

The section of the creed on Jesus Christ is structured like the church's ancient baptismal fonts, with steps descending into the water and steps ascending from it. Jesus came down from heaven, suffered and died, then was buried and descended into the underworld. He then rose from the dead, ascended into heaven, and is enthroned at the right hand of the Father. Descending not only into the created world but deeper and deeper into the depths of human sin and death, he defeats all the powers that hold humanity in bondage. He then rises from the depths in victory and claims his power and dominion over the whole created world.

In his letter, Paul passes on the saving gospel through the words of a very ancient creed which he had received. The core of this good news is that "Christ died for our sins" and "was raised on the third day" (verses 3–4). Here is the essence of the Christian faith in a nutshell. This is what is "of first importance." This supremely important core of belief insists that Christ died and was raised "in accordance with the scriptures." There is no single text that explicitly anticipates the Messiah's death and resurrection, but the earliest Christian tradition realized that the witness of the entire Old Testament anticipated this saving event. God's care for creation, fidelity to the covenant, unwavering love for his people, and his power over all opposing forces led to the liberating death and resurrection of the Lord. God's rescue of humanity from sin and death through Christ is the final phase of the story of salvation for ancient Israel.

The list of witnesses to the appearances of the risen Christ is an indication that the resurrection was real (verses 5–7). Neither Paul nor the early community thought that the resurrection was simply an ineffable, subjective experience or hallucination. His enumeration of a large though finite number of witnesses, noting that most were still living, indicates that there was a convincing number willing to testify that they had encountered Jesus alive.

Paul then begins an extended discussion of resurrection because some in the Corinthian church were saying there is no resurrection from the dead (verse 12). Paul develops his argument gently and thoroughly. If there is no resurrection from the death, then Christ himself cannot have been raised.

And if Christ has not been raised, then the apostles have been talking empty nonsense, and those who believed them have believed empty nonsense. In which case, Christians are liars who misrepresent God, there is no forgiveness of sins, and those who have died as Christians are simply lost. The Christian gospel stands or falls with the resurrection of the dead. Without the resurrection, Christianity is only a system of delusions and futile human fantasy, leaving its adherents "most to be pitied" (verse 19).

Sweeping away all the gloomy hypothetical consequences that follow from denying the resurrection, Paul triumphantly declares: "But in fact Christ has been raised from the dead" (verse 20). As a Jew, Paul had expected the resurrection to be a corporate rising of all God's people at a future time that God would determine. To claim that only Jesus was raised from the dead, before all others and before the end of the age, seemed to go against the biblical expectation. Paul therefore uses the metaphor of the "first fruits," the first sheaf of the grain harvest waved at the Jewish feast of Weeks as a sign and promise that the remainder of the harvest is soon to come. By calling the risen Christ "the first fruits of those who have died," Paul indicates that he understood the resurrection of Christ as an anticipatory promise of the general resurrection of the dead.

We live now in the interval between Christ's resurrection and the day of Christ's coming, when the dead will be raised to life. The time of forgiveness, restoration, and victory over sin and death, promised by Israel's prophets and sages for the age to come, has already come upon the earth through the resurrection of Christ. The future age has already burst into the present age, so that we live now with a mixture of fulfillment and expectation. What happened when Christ rose from the tomb has made the world a different place and has given us the possibility to become a different kind of people.

Reflection and Discussion

- Is Paul convincing when he says that the resurrection is the bedrock of Christianity? Why is the resurrection from the dead the saving event upon which all the other truths of faith stand or fall?

- Paul's image of the "first fruits" indicates the relationship of Christ's resurrection to our own. In what way is the present age a time of both fulfillment and expectation?

- Later in this same discourse on the resurrection, Paul asks rhetorically, "Where, O death, is your victory? Where, O death, is your sting?" In what way does the resurrection take away the sting of death?

- What can sometimes cause me to loosen my grip on the core of the gospel? What can I do to "hold firmly to the message"?

Prayer

Father of our Lord Jesus Christ, without the resurrection from the dead, I am trapped in sin and destined for eternal death. Give me a fresh experience of your merciful love today and help me to witness the grace you have poured into my life.

LESSON 16 | SESSION 4

So if you have been raised with Christ, seek the things that are above, where Christ is, seated at the right hand of God. COLOSSIANS 3:1

Ascended into Heaven and Seated at the Right Hand of the Father

ACTS 1:6–11 6 *So when they had come together, they asked him, "Lord, is this the time when you will restore the kingdom to Israel?"* 7 *He replied, "It is not for you to know the times or periods that the Father has set by his own authority.* 8 *But you will receive power when the Holy Spirit has come upon you; and you will be my witnesses in Jerusalem, in all Judea and Samaria, and to the ends of the earth."* 9 *When he had said this, as they were watching, he was lifted up, and a cloud took him out of their sight.* 10 *While he was going and they were gazing up toward heaven, suddenly two men in white robes stood by them.* 11 *They said, "Men of Galilee, why do you stand looking up toward heaven? This Jesus, who has been taken up from you into heaven, will come in the same way as you saw him go into heaven."*

ACTS 2:32–36 32 *"This Jesus God raised up, and of that all of us are witnesses.*
33 *Being therefore exalted at the right hand of God, and having received from the Father the promise of the Holy Spirit, he has poured out this that you both see and hear.* 34 *For David did not ascend into the heavens, but he himself says,*

> *'The Lord said to my Lord,*
> *"Sit at my right hand,*
> 35 *until I make your enemies your footstool."'*

36 *Therefore let the entire house of Israel know with certainty that God has made him both Lord and Messiah, this Jesus whom you crucified."*

COLOSSIANS 3:1–4 [1]*So if you have been raised with Christ, seek the things that are above, where Christ is, seated at the right hand of God.* [2]*Set your minds on things that are above, not on things that are on earth,* [3]*for you have died, and your life is hidden with Christ in God.* [4]*When Christ who is your life is revealed, then you also will be revealed with him in glory.*

The resurrection of Jesus is not a return to mortal life. No longer among the dead, Jesus, in his human nature and incarnate existence, now shares in the immortal existence of God. The New Testament writers express this truth in a number of different ways. The Acts of the Apostles says that Jesus was "lifted up," that a cloud took him out of the sight of the apostles and toward heaven. For the ancient worldview that saw the place of God as above the firmament, this spatial imagery effectively communicates the truth that Jesus now reigns with God's own life and power. But with the cosmology of today, we must avoid the inevitable literalism that suggests that Jesus went up into space. Instead, we must seek the fuller meaning and significance of this divine mystery.

Peter's speech in Acts proclaims that God raised Jesus up and exalted him at the right hand of the Father, the place of honor. Jesus now shares in God's royal power over creation, as stated in the first verse of Psalm 110: "The Lord says to my Lord, 'Sit at my right hand, until I make your enemies your footstool.'" Other passages in Acts and in Paul's writings say that God "exalted" and "glorified" Jesus. All of this terminology witnesses to the fact that Jesus is active and powerful in his church, even more so than during his earthly ministry. The fact that Jesus is no longer physically present with his followers anticipates the coming of the Holy Spirit and the Spirit-filled ministry of Jesus' followers in the church.

The paradox of Jesus' absence and presence expresses the reality of the early church experiencing the fulfillment of Jesus' promises. Jesus transcends the physical and material dimensions of earthly life. He must be "absent" from his disciples in his former manner so that he can be "present" to them in a more intimate and powerful way through the gift of the Holy Spirit. The creed's statements about the exaltation of Jesus express the truth about Jesus now for the church. His ascension and glorification are the foundation for the church's worship and its service in his name.

The ascension of Jesus instills into our lives an eternal purpose and heavenly perspective. Paul urges us, "Set your minds on things that are above, not on things that are on earth" (Col 3:2). Our future has meaning because Christ reigns in heaven. Although we should always point our lives toward our transcendent destiny, we must not "stand looking up toward heaven" (Acts 1:11). Rather, we look forward to the great mission that Jesus has given to his church. The Christian view of the world is filled with possibilities because its future is under the sovereign rule of the ascended Lord. As Christ reigns from heaven, he rules his church through the word and sacraments he has given to her. With Christ's authority and direction, the church turns to its work of evangelizing the nations, baptizing, and teaching. Under his reign, the kingdom will come on earth as it is in heaven. We will be ruled under the eye of heavenly judgment until one day we will give an accounting of what we have done under his reign.

Reflection and Discussion

- In the glorified Christ, who remains forever both human and divine, we have all been given admission to the heart of the Trinity. How does this truth give purpose and confidence to my life?

- Although Jesus is physically absent from the world as the exalted Lord, how does he manifest his presence to me? How can I more fully witness to his presence with me and with his church?

Prayer

Lord Jesus, I believe that you have ascended to heaven and now sit at the right hand of the Father, interceding for your people and ruling over creation. As we await your return in glory, teach me to be trustful and confident in you and your plans for me.

LESSON 17 SESSION 4

The hour is coming when all who are in their graves will hear his voice and will come out—those who have done good, to the resurrection of life, and those who have done evil, to the resurrection of condemnation. JOHN 5:28–29

He Will Come Again in Glory

MATTHEW 25:31–46 31*"When the Son of Man comes in his glory, and all the angels with him, then he will sit on the throne of his glory.* 32*All the nations will be gathered before him, and he will separate people one from another as a shepherd separates the sheep from the goats,* 33*and he will put the sheep at his right hand and the goats at the left.* 34*Then the king will say to those at his right hand, 'Come, you that are blessed by my Father, inherit the kingdom prepared for you from the foundation of the world;* 35*for I was hungry and you gave me food, I was thirsty and you gave me something to drink, I was a stranger and you welcomed me,* 36*I was naked and you gave me clothing, I was sick and you took care of me, I was in prison and you visited me.'* 37*Then the righteous will answer him, 'Lord, when was it that we saw you hungry and gave you food, or thirsty and gave you something to drink?* 38*And when was it that we saw you a stranger and welcomed you, or naked and gave you clothing?* 39*And when was it that we saw you sick or in prison and visited you?'* 40*And the king will answer them, 'Truly I tell you, just as you did it to one of the least of these who are members of my family, you did it to me.'* 41*Then he will say to those at his left hand, 'You that are accursed, depart from me into the eternal fire prepared for the devil and his angels;* 42*for I was hungry and you gave me no food, I was thirsty and you gave me nothing to drink,* 43*I was a stranger and you did not welcome me, naked and you did not give me clothing, sick and in*

prison and you did not visit me.' [44]*Then they also will answer, 'Lord, when was it*
that we saw you hungry or thirsty or a stranger or naked or sick or in prison, and
did not take care of you?' [45]*Then he will answer them, 'Truly I tell you, just as you*
did not do it to one of the least of these, you did not do it to me.' [46]*And these will go*
away into eternal punishment, but the righteous into eternal life."

JOHN 5:22–29 [22]*The Father judges no one but has given all judgment to the Son,*
[23]*so that all may honor the Son just as they honor the Father. Anyone who does*
not honor the Son does not honor the Father who sent him. [24]*Very truly, I tell you,*
anyone who hears my word and believes him who sent me has eternal life, and does
not come under judgment, but has passed from death to life.

[25]*"Very truly, I tell you, the hour is coming, and is now here, when the dead*
will hear the voice of the Son of God, and those who hear will live. [26]*For just as*
the Father has life in himself, so he has granted the Son also to have life in him-
self; [27]*and he has given him authority to execute judgment, because he is the Son*
of Man. [28]*Do not be astonished at this; for the hour is coming when all who are*
in their graves will hear his voice [29]*and will come out—those who have done*
good, to the resurrection of life, and those who have done evil, to the resurrection
of condemnation.

The Old Testament presents the Creator as the judge of all his creation, continually seeking justice on the earth. The Torah and the prophets express confidence that God decides fairly between human beings and acts to rectify the wrongs that people do to each other. God is the one who sees into the heart, and therefore he is able to base his judgment not on appearances but on true intention. God's justice is not just a matter of tallying up good and bad deeds, but rather of passionate involvement in the world to set it aright. God's final judgment, however, will not be given until "the day of the Lord," when God will restore the divine order and bring about a new age of blessings.

The New Testament testifies that the divine judgment of the world will take place in and through Jesus Christ. The one who once came to earth in great humility will one day come again in glory. The one who redeemed the world through his cross and resurrection will judge the living and the dead. According to Paul: "All of us must appear before the judgment seat of Christ, so that each may receive recompense for what has been done in the body, whether good or evil" (2 Cor 5:10). Then God's saving plan for the world will reach its completion, and the kingdom of God will be established in its fullness.

In his final discourse in Matthew's gospel, Jesus teaches his disciples how to live during the interval between his ascension and his coming again. Through parables and teachings, he demonstrates the necessity of alertness and faithfulness. The discourse ends with the great judgment scene which presents Jesus as the messianic king who will come in glory as all the nations are assembled before him. With this scene Jesus adds deeds of compassion as requirements for those who wait for his return in glory. He repeats the mention of those who are hungry, thirsty, away from home, naked, sick, and imprisoned a total of four times in this scene. This repetition imprints these needy least ones on the minds of his listeners as Jesus leads them to understand that he himself is present in his suffering brothers and sisters. The conclusion stresses the everlasting significance of the decision whether to help them.

In John's gospel, Jesus teaches his disciples that the divine judgment expected for the final age is already happening in his own ministry. Eternal life is available in the present for those who hear the word of Jesus and believe in the Father who sent him (John 5:24). This belief in God's revelation demands a changed life, expressed in deeds and not merely words. The future resurrection of the dead will reveal and confirm the choices that people have already made to receive or reject the life that has been offered to them. They will rise to the "resurrection of life" or the "resurrection of condemnation" based on whether they have "done good" or "done evil."

The article of the creed that states, "He will come in glory to judge the living and the dead," infuses purpose and direction into our personal lives within God's plan of salvation history. It convinces us that our lives are reaching toward a final goal and that everything we do has an eternal meaning. The countless acts of kindness and love that we do throughout our lives are not fleeting but have an everlasting purpose. We can remain patient and faithful because we know that the Lord we serve will one day bring all things to justice and bring forth the new creation in all its fullness.

Reflection and Discussion

- As Jesus speaks about those who are hungry, thirsty, away from home, naked, sick, and imprisoned, what is the common element in all of these people? What would be another type of person Jesus might mention today?

- In light of Jesus' judgment of the nations, how might his teaching challenge my nation's policies and actions regarding poverty, nutrition, health care, prisons, or immigration? How can I be an agent of change in our society today?

- In what sense is eternal life both a present and a future reality? What are the qualities of my present life that seem to be a sharing in eternal life? What parts of my present life would I want to last forever?

Prayer

Lord of all the nations, thank you for redeeming me so that I can live with confidence in the future you have planned for me. Help me to see your presence in those who are hungry, thirsty, away from home, naked, sick, and imprisoned.

"See, the home of God is among mortals. He will dwell with them; they will be his peoples, and God himself will be with them; he will wipe every tear from their eyes." REVELATION 21:3–4

His Kingdom Will Have No End

REVELATION 20:11—21:7 11 *Then I saw a great white throne and the one who sat*
on it; the earth and the heaven fled from his presence, and no place was found for
them. 12 *And I saw the dead, great and small, standing before the throne, and books*
were opened. Also another book was opened, the book of life. And the dead were
judged according to their works, as recorded in the books. 13 *And the sea gave up the*
dead that were in it, Death and Hades gave up the dead that were in them, and all
were judged according to what they had done. 14 *Then Death and Hades were thrown*
into the lake of fire. This is the second death, the lake of fire; 15 *and anyone whose*
name was not found written in the book of life was thrown into the lake of fire.

21 1 *Then I saw a new heaven and a new earth; for the first heaven and the first*
earth had passed away, and the sea was no more. 2 *And I saw the holy city, the new*
Jerusalem, coming down out of heaven from God, prepared as a bride adorned for
her husband. 3 *And I heard a loud voice from the throne saying,*

"See, the home of God is among mortals.
He will dwell with them;
they will be his peoples,
and God himself will be with them;
4 *he will wipe every tear from their eyes.*
Death will be no more;
mourning and crying and pain will be no more,
for the first things have passed away."

[5]*And the one who was seated on the throne said, "See, I am making all things new." Also he said, "Write this, for these words are trustworthy and true."* [6]*Then he said to me, "It is done! I am the Alpha and the Omega, the beginning and the end. To the thirsty I will give water as a gift from the spring of the water of life.* [7]*Those who conquer will inherit these things, and I will be their God and they will be my children."*

Jesus began his ministry by announcing that the kingdom of God has come near, and he commissioned his disciples to proclaim the same message. God's kingdom is not a place but rather the condition in which God and creation are in a right relationship. This messianic kingdom, which the prophets had proclaimed and for which Israel was waiting, would bring the definitive state of justice, love, and peace to all people. Jesus teaches his followers to pray for the coming of the kingdom on earth as it is in heaven. His powerful deeds of healing and liberation demonstrate that the rule of God is breaking into the world. His parables express the fact that the kingdom is already present in mystery because the final age is with us and the renewal of the world is irreversibly under way.

The last visions of the book of Revelation express the final destruction of evil and death followed by God's eternal reign. All the dead come to life and stand before the "great white throne" of God's judgment. "The great and the small"—all come; there are no exceptions and no deferrals. All are judged according to their works (20:11–13). Even though all have been enrolled in the "book of life" by God's grace—that is, invited to share in eternal life—everyone is still judged according to how they have responded during their lifetime to that noble call.

Following the judgment, God's kingdom is described with beautiful images of creation perfected by its Creator, "a new heaven and a new earth" (21:1). Human language is incapable of expressing, and human imagination is incapable of perceiving, the perfection of God's reign over creation. Yet, this does not hinder the writer from using a variety of metaphors to articulate the wonders of God's final plan for the world.

In this renewed creation, God dwells with this people, making his home with humanity and caring for this people in all their needs. He definitively puts an end to the pains of suffering and death (21:3–4). He is "the Alpha and the Omega" (21:6), the one who created all things and the one who brings about the completion and perfection of all.

Like the Gospel of John, the book of Revelation indicates that the new creation for which we hope has already begun in the saving work of Jesus Christ. God is already "making all things new" (21:5). In Christ we have already begun to experience God's presence, his comfort, and new life. With the coming of Jesus, God has already begun to dwell with the human race. We have already experienced God's life-giving water flowing from within us. We can already experience the tender parental love of God as his sons and daughters. Even if our experience of God's presence is often faint or fragmentary now, we can find consolation and courage in this vision because we know that what we have experienced dimly will embrace us completely.

The Creed demonstrates that the world's salvation through Jesus Christ embraces the past, present, and future. From the standpoint of our earthly realm, we know that the life of Jesus in the flesh and his death on the cross are in the past. His resurrection, ascension, and eternal rule is the present reality for believers. And his coming again as judge of the living and the dead is the future which we await. Yet, in the divine realm there is only an eternal present. Jesus is continually offering himself in sacrifice to the Father, a reality made present in the eucharistic liturgy of the church. Likewise, the coming judgment and kingdom is brought into the present in sacramental worship because it is eternally accomplished in the timeless and everlasting realm of God.

The saving actions of Christ—past, present, and future—potentially include all humanity. His descent into humanity is for us, and his ascent into glory includes us. The Fathers of the church taught that the whole point of the incarnation of God is the deification of humanity. As St. Athanasius declared, "God became man, so that man might become God" (Athanasius, *De Incarnatione* 54:13).

This deification of humanity must not be taken in a literal way, as if we become God. Yet, it is far more than a mere metaphor. The mystery of Christ's dying and rising becomes present and effective for us through the church's sacramental liturgy. Like the Paschal Mystery, the liturgy is one continuing movement of descent and ascent. Through the work of the Holy Spirit in the church, we are plunged into the stream of salvation history, and we ascend with Christ to the throne of God's grace. Through our taking part in the dying of Jesus by dying to sin and in the resurrection of Jesus by being born to new life, we become members of Christ's body and share in his life.

There is an analogy between the incarnation of God and the deification of humanity, which is most clearly indicated in the prayer of the priest during the preparation of the gifts at Mass when he mixes the water with the wine and says, "By the mystery of this water and wine, may we come to share in the divinity of Christ, who humbled himself to share in our humanity." As St. Athanasius preached, "By the participation of the Spirit, we become communicants in the divine nature… For this reason, those in whom the Spirit dwells are divinized" (Athanasius, *Ep. Serap.* 1, 24). Deification by grace, that is, becoming sons and daughters of God in the Only Begotten Son of God, is the whole point of the incarnation, passion, death, resurrection, and exaltation of the Lord.

Reflection and Discussion

- God has promised that we will live forever, free from fear, pain, sin, or death. In what ways does this promise give me courage and hope? What glimpses has God given me of the joys that await me?

- One of the earliest eucharistic acclamations of the church, expressed in the final words of the book of Revelation (22:20), is "Come, Lord Jesus!" In what way is the eucharistic liturgy an anticipation of all that God has promised us in his eternal kingdom?

Prayer

God of compassionate love, you are the beginning and the end. You have created me and you will make me new. May your Spirit move within me to renew my life so that I may live in joyful hope.

SUGGESTIONS FOR FACILITATORS, GROUP SESSION 4

1. Welcome group members and ask if anyone has any questions, announcements, or requests.

2. You may want to pray this prayer as a group:
   Lord Jesus, who descended into the depths of human suffering and ascended into heaven to reign with the Father, we believe that we have been reconciled to you by your cross and experience salvation through your resurrection. As we await your return in glory, teach us to see your presence in those who are hungry, thirsty, away from home, naked, sick, and imprisoned. May your Spirit move within us to renew our lives and to give us trustful confidence and joyful hope in your plans for us.

3. Ask one or both of the following questions:
   - What is the most difficult part of this study for you?
   - What insights stand out to you from the lessons this week?

4. Discuss lessons 13 through 18. Choose one or more of the questions for reflection and discussion from each lesson to discuss as a group. You may want to ask group members which question was most challenging or helpful for them as you review each lesson.

5. Keep the discussion moving but allow time for the questions that provoke the best discussion. Encourage the group members to use "I" language in their responses.

6. After talking over each lesson, instruct group members to complete lessons 19 through 24 on their own during the six days before the next group meeting. They should write out their own answers to the questions as preparation for next week's session.

7. Ask the group what encouragement they need for the coming week. Ask the members to pray for the needs of one another during the week.

8. Conclude by praying aloud together the prayer at the end of one of the lessons discussed. You may choose to conclude the prayer by asking members to pray aloud any requests they may have.

LESSON 19 SESSION 5

“The Advocate, the Holy Spirit, whom the Father will send in my name, will teach you everything, and remind you of all that I have said to you.” JOHN 14:26

I Believe in the Holy Spirit

JOHN 14:15–27 *15“If you love me, you will keep my commandments. 16And I will*
ask the Father, and he will give you another Advocate, to be with you forever. 17This
is the Spirit of truth, whom the world cannot receive, because it neither sees him
nor knows him. You know him, because he abides with you, and he will be in you.

18“I will not leave you orphaned; I am coming to you. 19In a little while the
world will no longer see me, but you will see me; because I live, you also will live.
20On that day you will know that I am in my Father, and you in me, and I in you.
21They who have my commandments and keep them are those who love me; and
those who love me will be loved by my Father, and I will love them and reveal
myself to them.” 22Judas (not Iscariot) said to him, “Lord, how is it that you will
reveal yourself to us, and not to the world?” 23Jesus answered him, “Those who love
me will keep my word, and my Father will love them, and we will come to them
and make our home with them. 24Whoever does not love me does not keep my
words; and the word that you hear is not mine, but is from the Father who sent me.

25“I have said these things to you while I am still with you. 26But the Advocate,
the Holy Spirit, whom the Father will send in my name, will teach you everything,
and remind you of all that I have said to you. 27Peace I leave with you; my peace I
give to you. I do not give to you as the world gives. Do not let your hearts be troubled, and do not let them be afraid.”

As the earthly life of Jesus draws to a close and as he prepares his disciples for his departure and return to the Father, Jesus promises his disciples that he will not leave them orphans (verse 18). Because they have been born from above and have become children of the Father, they will experience the loving intimacy of God's family even more closely: "You will know that I am in my Father, and you in me, and I in you" (verse 20). Even though Jesus is departing from them, he promises that he will come to them and remain with them through his Holy Spirit. This abiding presence of Jesus, even in his absence, is the work of the Spirit, whom Jesus promises will be "with" and "in" his disciples (verse 17). In this new era of the Spirit, the living Jesus will be closer to his disciples than ever before.

In this section of John's gospel, Jesus calls the Holy Spirit the "Paraclete," a Greek word that literally means "one called to the side of another." Paraclete is translated in various ways: Advocate, Helper, Counselor, Comforter, and Consoler (verses 16, 26). The Spirit will do for the disciples what Jesus himself did for them when he was living in their midst—especially teaching and encouraging them. The Paraclete will illuminate the revelation from God that Jesus brought and apply it to the ever-changing needs of the community.

The Paraclete is also called "the Spirit of truth" (verse 17). Jesus came to reveal to us the ultimate truth: the truth of the Father's love experienced by Jesus and manifested in his life, death, and resurrection. We are invited to participate in this truth by becoming one with Jesus through faith. The Spirit of truth is instinctively and interiorly experienced as an abiding presence by those who follow the glorified Jesus. Through believing in Jesus, loving him, and keeping his commandments, the disciples receive the Holy Spirit. The physical departure of Jesus does not end his real presence or the ongoing revelation of God in Jesus.

This presence of the Holy Spirit, "whom the world cannot receive," is unable to be seen in the usual and worldly sense of the term (verse 17). For that reason, Judas asks Jesus why the disciples and the world see things so differently (verse 22). Jesus explains that those who do not accept God's loving invitation cannot experience the Spirit of truth, the ongoing presence and revelation of God. The Spirit is first of all a gift from God, but a gift that must be accepted through one's loving, active response to God's word. Contrary to outward appearances, Jesus and the Father will make their home with the disciples (verse 23) in and through the Holy Spirit, who will be with them forever.

The effect of the Spirit's work within believers is a profound sense of peace, well-being, and confidence, the kind of peace that the world cannot give (verse 27). The *pax Romana* (Roman peace), secured by the emperor Augustus during the lifetime of Jesus, was obtained and maintained by military might. The peace given by Jesus, in contrast, was not obtained by inflicting violence or maintained with force. This peace does not go away even in the midst of life's most difficult struggles.

Reflection and Discussion

- As Jesus spends much of his final discourse preparing his followers for life in the age of the Spirit, what are some of the changes Jesus emphasizes for the church after his departure?

- Since the Spirit of truth brings to light the meaning and significance of the revelation given by Jesus, in what ways have I experienced the Holy Spirit teaching me and reminding me as I study the Scriptures?

- Jesus reassures his disciples, "Do not let your hearts be troubled, and do not let them be afraid." In what areas of my life do I need to call on the Holy Spirit to give me confidence and peace? How can I open my life to the Spirit's work?

Prayer

Glorified Christ, send me your Advocate, the Spirit of truth, to abide with me and live in me. May your Spirit guide me as I read the Scriptures and continue your revealing work within me.

Indeed, to this very day whenever Moses is read, a veil lies over their minds; but when one turns to the Lord, the veil is removed.

2 CORINTHIANS 3:15–16

Holy Spirit, the Lord

JOHN 16:7–15 7*Nevertheless I tell you the truth: it is to your advantage that I go
away, for if I do not go away, the Advocate will not come to you; but if I go, I will
send him to you.* 8*And when he comes, he will prove the world wrong about sin and
righteousness and judgment:* 9*about sin, because they do not believe in me;* 10*about
righteousness, because I am going to the Father and you will see me no longer;*
11*about judgment, because the ruler of this world has been condemned.*

12*"I still have many things to say to you, but you cannot bear them now.* 13*When
the Spirit of truth comes, he will guide you into all the truth; for he will not speak
on his own, but will speak whatever he hears, and he will declare to you the things
that are to come.* 14*He will glorify me, because he will take what is mine and declare
it to you.* 15*All that the Father has is mine. For this reason I said that he will take
what is mine and declare it to you.*

2 CORINTHIANS 3:12–18 12*Since, then, we have such a hope, we act with great
boldness,* 13*not like Moses, who put a veil over his face to keep the people of Israel
from gazing at the end of the glory that was being set aside.* 14*But their minds were
hardened. Indeed, to this very day, when they hear the reading of the old covenant,
that same veil is still there, since only in Christ is it set aside.* 15*Indeed, to this very
day whenever Moses is read, a veil lies over their minds;* 16*but when one turns to
the Lord, the veil is removed.* 17*Now the Lord is the Spirit, and where the Spirit of
the Lord is, there is freedom.* 18*And all of us, with unveiled faces, seeing the glory
of the Lord as though reflected in a mirror, are being transformed into the same
image from one degree of glory to another; for this comes from the Lord, the Spirit.*

The human experience of continual parting from loved ones would fill our lives with constant sorrow were it not for the hope-filled existence we have been given in Jesus Christ. Even though he must depart from his disciples, amazingly he tells them, "It is to your advantage that I go away" (John 16:7). The earthly attachment of Jesus and his disciples had to end, but only to create a bond that would never end, an attachment of the disciples to Jesus and the Father through the Holy Spirit.

The Paraclete (Advocate) makes the glorified Jesus present to us. The Spirit is the eternal presence of the divine Christ with believers, the fulfillment of his promises to dwell with his disciples. Though it might seem attractive to have been with Jesus during his earthly life, there is no doubt that Jesus is more present to us now in the Spirit than he ever was to his disciples during his earthly life. In those days, Jesus lived "with" his disciples; after he is glorified, Jesus lives "in" his disciples through the Spirit.

The Spirit of truth will guide believers "into all the truth" (John 16:13). If our understanding of Jesus were limited to only what Jesus was able to convey to his followers during his public life on earth, our belief would be as inadequate as that of the disciples before the resurrection. But the Holy Spirit enlightens disciples to understand and experience the truth of Christ much more richly. Because of the Spirit, Jesus is not a distant figure from the past; he is the living Lord of our lives. Through the Spirit of truth, the whole mystery of Jesus, his words, actions, death, and resurrection, will be more completely comprehended, interiorized, and lived.

The gift of the Spirit signals a new stage in the history of salvation. After the resurrection of Jesus and before his final coming in glory, the community of disciples experiences Christ in the sacramental worship and Spirit-guided teaching of the church. During this age of the church, the Holy Spirit reminds disciples of all that Jesus has said and declares "the things that are to come." The disciples' journey "into all the truth" is not yet complete. The "many things" (John 16:12) that Jesus did not tell his disciples during his earthly life will gradually be revealed through the work of the Spirit in the ongoing life of Christ's church.

In Paul's writings, he develops a contrast between the glory of God's presence that was only temporary in God's revelation to Moses and the permanent glory that shines on the face of the risen Lord. He asserts that the veil of obscurity that covers God's revelation to Moses is lifted by the Spirit so that God's revelation may be clearly understood (2 Cor 3:15–16). The title "Lord" points to the deep unity between the Spirit experienced by Christians in the church and the Lord God who created all things and the Lord Jesus who reigns with the Father in heaven.

To declare that "the Lord is the Spirit" (2 Cor 3:17) is to assert that the Holy Spirit is God. God's Spirit points us to the Father and the Son, revealing himself as the Spirit of the Father and of the Son. As the Holy Spirit lifts the veil from our faces, we are progressively transformed into God's image.

Reflection and Discussion

- Why was Jesus unable to say to his disciples many of the things he had to tell them (John 16:12)? In what way does the Holy Spirit, present in the community of disciples, guide the church "into all the truth" (John 16:13)?

- As the Holy Spirit uncovers the veil of the Scriptures' obscurity for us, we are progressively transformed into the Lord's image. In what ways do I experience the transforming work of God's Spirit as I continue to study God's word?

- Through the presence of the Holy Spirit, Jesus is more present with me now than he was with his disciples on earth. In what ways do I experience this Spirit-guided intimacy with Jesus in my own life?

Prayer

Come, Holy Spirit, empower your church to transform our world with your truth. Guide me into the fullness of truth and help me to comprehend the mystery of Christ in all its richness and depth.

LESSON 21 SESSION 5

"Repent, and be baptized every one of you in the name of Jesus Christ so that your sins may be forgiven; and you will receive the gift of the Holy Spirit." ACTS 2:38

Holy Spirit, the Giver of Life

ACTS 2:1–13 [1]*When the day of Pentecost had come, they were all together in one place.* [2]*And suddenly from heaven there came a sound like the rush of a violent wind, and it filled the entire house where they were sitting.* [3]*Divided tongues, as of fire, appeared among them, and a tongue rested on each of them.* [4]*All of them were filled with the Holy Spirit and began to speak in other languages, as the Spirit gave them ability.*

[5]*Now there were devout Jews from every nation under heaven living in Jerusalem.* [6]*And at this sound the crowd gathered and was bewildered, because each one heard them speaking in the native language of each.* [7]*Amazed and astonished, they asked, "Are not all these who are speaking Galileans?* [8]*And how is it that we hear, each of us, in our own native language?* [9]*Parthians, Medes, Elamites, and residents of Mesopotamia, Judea and Cappadocia, Pontus and Asia,* [10]*Phrygia and Pamphylia, Egypt and the parts of Libya belonging to Cyrene, and visitors from Rome, both Jews and proselytes,* [11]*Cretans and Arabs—in our own languages we hear them speaking about God's deeds of power."* [12]*All were amazed and perplexed, saying to one another, "What does this mean?"* [13]*But others sneered and said, "They are filled with new wine."*

ACTS 2:37–42 [37]*Now when they heard this, they were cut to the heart and said to Peter and to the other apostles, "Brothers, what should we do?"* [38]*Peter said to* *them, "Repent, and be baptized every one of you in the name of Jesus Christ so that your sins may be forgiven; and you will receive the gift of the Holy Spirit.* [39]*For the promise is for you, for your children, and for all who are far away, everyone whom the Lord our God calls to him."* [40]*And he testified with many other arguments and exhorted them, saying, "Save yourselves from this corrupt generation."* [41]*So those who welcomed his message were baptized, and that day about three thousand persons were added.* [42]*They devoted themselves to the apostles' teaching and fellowship, to the breaking of bread and the prayers.*

Orthodox Christians celebrate Pentecost by adorning their churches with flowers and green foliage. Bringing greenery of all kinds to the church expresses the truth that the Holy Spirit is the "giver of life" and that because of the Spirit, the church is always young and never grows old. The verdant life that fills the church celebrates not just biological life but the divine life that flows into the church from the Godhead. This life from above is immortal and everlasting.

From the beginnings of Scripture, we see that the foremost activity of God's Spirit is presiding over the genesis of new life. The Spirit hovered over the primordial waters to draw forth from them an orderly evolution of new life—first the sea creatures, then the creatures of the sky and land, and finally human beings. God breathed his Spirit, the breath of life, into the human creature and he became a living being. From these beginnings, God's Spirit has been present at each new stage of developing new life for God's people.

In the writings of Luke, Pentecost is the last of three stages in Jesus' relationship with the Spirit. The first begins with his conception in Mary through the power of the Holy Spirit (Luke 1:35). The second begins with Jesus' baptism, when he is anointed with the Spirit and confirmed as the Messiah (Luke 3:22). The third begins with his death and resurrection, and it is unfolded in his ascension and Pentecost. The one who was first filled with the Holy Spirit now sends the Spirit and clothes his disciples "with power from on high" (Luke 24:49).

John the Baptist had announced that Jesus would baptize "with the Holy Spirit and fire" (Luke 3:16). But Jesus himself would first undergo his own baptism of fire in his passion and death for us. Because Jesus was baptized with fire in the destructive power of the cross, the fire of Pentecost became the power of

God's gracious gift to his church. Pentecost is intimately related to the saving life of Christ and is the culmination of his resurrection, exaltation, and glorification.

The day of Pentecost began with an eruption of sound like a rushing wind. The same divine wind that swept over the waters at the beginning of creation was producing a new creation. As the prophets had declared, God was putting "a new spirit," God's own Spirit, within his people so that their life may be renewed (Ezek 36:26–27). The effects of sin, represented by the confusion of Babel (Gen 11:1–9), began to be reversed at Pentecost. At Babel, the one language of humanity became confused so that people could not understand one another and so they scattered over the face of the earth. At Pentecost, the one gospel began to be heard and understood in the language of "every nation under heaven." The fiery "tongues" became the gift of other tongues (languages) as they began to speak under the promptings of the Holy Spirit (verse 4). Once again, God's Spirit was bringing order out of confusion, creation out of chaos, so that the church could witness the gospel all over the world.

Not only was God creating his people anew, but the Holy Spirit was resting upon each person as they began to speak fearlessly. The first to speak was Peter (verse 38). The same Spirit that God blew into the newly formed Adam to create a living being now breathed life into this once cowardly disciple and created a new man. The same Peter, who only a few weeks before could not speak up when his master was on trial, now proclaims the message of Christ in the power of the Holy Spirit.

Reflection and Discussion

- How does Luke indicate that Pentecost is God's work of new creation and the birth of the church?

- What is the relationship of the feasts of the Annunciation, the Baptism of Jesus, and Pentecost? Why is Pentecost the conclusion of the liturgical season of Easter?

- At the Epiclesis of the Eucharistic Prayer, the priest invokes the Holy Spirit over the gifts of bread and wine in these words: "Make holy, therefore, these gifts, we pray, by sending down your Spirit upon them like the dewfall." How does this image convey the truth that the Holy Spirit is the giver of life?

- In what ways was Peter transformed by the power of the Holy Spirit? What gift could I ask of God's Spirit to bring me renewed life?

Prayer

Come, Holy Spirit, come as you did on that first Pentecost to give life to your church. Continue your work of renewal within me and kindle in me the fire of your divine love.

LESSON 22 SESSION 5

"Being therefore exalted at the right hand of God, and having received from the Father the promise of the Holy Spirit, he has poured out this that you both see and hear." ACTS 2:33

Who Proceeds from the Father and the Son

JOHN 15:26–27 26*"When the Advocate comes, whom I will send to you from the Father, the Spirit of truth who comes from the Father, he will testify on my behalf.* 27*You also are to testify because you have been with me from the beginning."*

ACTS 2:32–33 32*"This Jesus God raised up, and of that all of us are witnesses.* 33*Being therefore exalted at the right hand of God, and having received from the Father the promise of the Holy Spirit, he has poured out this that you both see and hear."*

ROMANS 8:1–17 1*There is therefore now no condemnation for those who are in Christ Jesus.* 2*For the law of the Spirit of life in Christ Jesus has set you free from the law of sin and of death.* 3*For God has done what the law, weakened by the flesh, could not do: by sending his own Son in the likeness of sinful flesh, and to deal with sin, he condemned sin in the flesh,* 4*so that the just requirement of the law might be fulfilled in us, who walk not according to the flesh but according to the Spirit.* 5*For those who live according to the flesh set their minds on the things of the flesh, but those who live according to the Spirit set their minds on the things of the Spirit.* 6*To set the mind on the flesh is death, but to set the mind on the Spirit is life and peace.* 7*For this reason the mind that is set on the flesh is hostile to God; it does not submit to God's law—indeed it cannot,* 8*and those who are in the flesh cannot please God.*

9*But you are not in the flesh; you are in the Spirit, since the Spirit of God dwells*
in you. Anyone who does not have the Spirit of Christ does not belong to him. 10*But*
if Christ is in you, though the body is dead because of sin, the Spirit is life because
of righteousness. 11*If the Spirit of him who raised Jesus from the dead dwells in you,*
he who raised Christ from the dead will give life to your mortal bodies also through
his Spirit that dwells in you.

12*So then, brothers and sisters, we are debtors, not to the flesh, to live according*
*to the flesh—*13*for if you live according to the flesh, you will die; but if by the Spirit*
you put to death the deeds of the body, you will live. 14*For all who are led by the*
Spirit of God are children of God. 15*For you did not receive a spirit of slavery to*
fall back into fear, but you have received a spirit of adoption. When we cry, "Abba!
Father!" 16*it is that very Spirit bearing witness with our spirit that we are children*
of God, 17*and if children, then heirs, heirs of God and joint heirs with Christ—if,*
in fact, we suffer with him so that we may also be glorified with him.

The original Nicene Creed professed belief in the Holy Spirit "who proceeds from the Father," an effort to express the truths of Scripture and reaffirm the divinity of God's Spirit. The text most determinative of this creedal statement is from Jesus' final discourse in John's gospel: "When the Advocate comes, whom I will send to you from the Father, the Spirit of truth who comes from the Father, he will testify on my behalf" (John 15:26). Here, it seems clear that the Holy Spirit comes "from the Father." As the Son is "begotten" by the Father, the Holy Spirit "proceeds" from the Father. The Son and the Spirit are not made by the Father but in some way come from the Father.

By confessing that the Holy Spirit proceeds "from the Father," which remains the creedal confession of the Orthodox Church today, believers affirm that the Father is the first origin of the Spirit. The Holy Spirit proceeds "from" the Father "through" the Son. The New Testament testimony to the Holy Spirit, however, is splendidly ambiguous. Other theologians, especially in the West, believed that the full testimony of Scripture demonstrates that the Spirit comes equally from the Father "and the Son" (in Latin, *Filioque*). For example, Peter's speech in Acts describes the Holy Spirit proceeding from both the Father and the Son. "Having received from the Father the promise of the Holy Spirit," the glorified Christ "has poured out" the Spirit upon God's people (Acts 2:33). Because the

Son as much as the Father seems to be the origin of the Holy Spirit, the Catholic Church added the phrase "and the Son" to the Creed in the sixth century.

Paul's multiple titles for the Holy Spirit, sometimes the "Spirit of God" and other times the "Spirit of Christ" (Rom 8:9), adds to the lack of precise language in Scripture to express the relationships of the Father, Son, and Holy Spirit. The church in the East argues that the oneness of God is affirmed by stating that the Father is the single font of divinity in the Trinity. The church in the West holds that, since the Son is "consubstantial with the Father," the procession of the Holy Spirit must be common to both the Father and the Son. These variations express a legitimate complementarity in our attempts to express the mystery of the Trinity in human language.

Paul's letter to the Romans describes the way that God integrates the saving power of Christ's death and resurrection into the internal lives of believers through the Holy Spirit. He contrasts life in the flesh, motivated by self-centered interests and oriented toward death, and life in the Spirit, empowered by God's liberating grace and oriented toward life and peace (Rom 8:5–6). The Christian life is not just an intellectual agreement with the teachings of Jesus or an external identification with his cause. Rather, it is an internal makeover by the Holy Spirit dwelling within the baptized believer. Through this transforming and vitalizing process, the Christian personally participates in divine life.

The Christian life ultimately consists of allowing "the Spirit of him who raised Jesus from the dead" to live within us (Rom 8:11). Because the same holy power that dwelt so completely in Jesus is now dwelling in us, God is able to completely reorient our lives. The vivifying energy of the Holy Spirit works within us now and continuously into the future, ultimately transforming even our bodies, making them like the body of the risen Christ. The life we now share in the Spirit, though still influenced by sin and death, is the life we will have in full at the final resurrection when God will renew the heavens and the earth.

Paul describes our incorporation into divine life through images of a family. If we are led by God's Spirit, we become "children of God" and are able to call upon God as "Abba! Father!" (Rom 8:15–16). Life under the domination of sin makes us worried, fearful slaves; life in the Spirit makes us trusting, confident children. With his Spirit within us, we share in all the privileges of Christ. We become God's adopted children and we become co-heirs with Christ of all the glory the Father has given the Son (Rom 8:17).

Reflection and Discussion

- What are some of the indications that one is living "in the flesh" or "in the Spirit"? What are some of the ways I have experienced greater freedom, joy, or peace as a result of the Holy Spirit's transforming work within me?

- Because attitudes that enhance or destroy life in a human family also build up or tear down the church, which mindsets devastate the church and which ones enhance its life?

- What are some of my privileges and responsibilities as a member of the family of God? What can I do to enhance the life of the church today?

Prayer

Come, Holy Spirit, free my life from the tyranny of sin and death so that I will be free for a life of witness and service. Live within my heart to make me a child of God and enable me to confidently cry out to God, my Father.

"Go therefore and make disciples of all nations, baptizing them in the name of the Father and of the Son and of the Holy Spirit." MATTHEW 28:19

Adored and Glorified with the Father and the Son

MATTHEW 28:16–20 16 *Now the eleven disciples went to Galilee, to the mountain*
to which Jesus had directed them. 17 *When they saw him, they worshiped him; but*
some doubted. 18 *And Jesus came and said to them, "All authority in heaven and on*
earth has been given to me. 19 *Go therefore and make disciples of all nations, bap-*
tizing them in the name of the Father and of the Son and of the Holy Spirit, 20 *and*
teaching them to obey everything that I have commanded you. And remember, I
am with you always, to the end of the age."

As God has revealed himself to the Israelites on the mountain, so the risen Jesus appears to his eleven disciples on the mountain in Galilee. At his appearance, "they worshiped him." As the Israelites worshiped God and received his revelation, the disciples adored the divine presence of Christ and prepared to receive the final revelation of Matthew's gospel. Yet, like the people of Israel, some of his disciples doubted, a word that connotes uncertainty and hesitation at this first encounter with the Risen One. This mixture of worship and doubt, of faith and indecision, is characteristic of Christian discipleship until the close of the age.

The risen Jesus proclaims the universality of the authority bestowed upon him by the Father and commissions his disciples to a worldwide mission. Jesus commands them to "go" to the nations. Their commission reflects the threefold mission of the church: evangelization, baptism, and teaching. The initial task is the proclamation of the good news. Then new disciples are brought into the life of the church through baptism. Finally, detailed teaching in the way of Christ must guide the new disciples.

But this entire mission of the disciples is possible only because of the final promise of the risen Lord: "I am with you always, to the end of the age." Although the responsibilities of disciples are daunting, the resources that are available to them in Jesus' authority and abiding presence are more than adequate for the task. Through the same Holy Spirit who empowered Jesus during his public life, the disciples will experience his living presence in his church. The presence of Jesus through his Spirit will give confidence to disciples in every age, guiding and confirming their decisions, as they await his coming again.

Although Scripture clearly demonstrates that the Father and the Son are worshiped by God's people, the language of worship is not explicitly used in Scripture with reference to the Holy Spirit. Yet, the early church recognized that the grace that comes to believers in the gift of the Holy Spirit is truly a share in the divine life and a participation in God's glory. The church grew to understand that what the New Testament says about the identity and work of the Spirit leads to the insight that the Holy Spirit is God. And because the Spirit is divine, it is indeed right to worship the Holy Spirit and to recognize in him the power and the presence of God. The Holy Spirit, "who with the Father and the Son is adored and glorified," is one and the same God as the Father and the Son.

This grand finale of Matthew's gospel is Trinitarian: the Father gives his authority to his Son, and the Son is present in the Holy Spirit to the church in every age. The whole history of salvation, the sending of the Son and the Holy Spirit by the Father, continues in the church. Into this mystery of the Trinity, Jesus tells his disciples to baptize: "in the name of the Father and of the Son and of the Holy Spirit" (verse 19). The whole Christian life is a communion with each of the divine persons, without in any way separating them. All who glorify the Father do so through the Son and in the Holy Spirit. Through the grace of baptism, we share in the life of the Trinity, here on earth in the obscurity of faith with its belief and its doubts, and after death completely in eternal light.

Reflection and Discussion

- What is the threefold task that the risen Christ gave to his disciples? In what ways does the church continue this mission today through the working of the Holy Spirit?

- What insights and experiences helped the early church to understand that the Holy Spirit is to be worshiped and glorified along with the Father and the Son?

- Making the sign of the cross, invoking the Father, Son, and Holy Spirit, is a succinct profession of faith in the blessed Trinity. How can I pray the sign of the cross less mechanically and as a conscious act of worship? What do I want to remember the next time I make the sign of the cross?

Prayer

Father, Son, and Holy Spirit, I believe that you are the one true God. I worship and glorify you, one unchanging God, revealing yourself as three divine persons. Thank you for creating me, for redeeming me, for sanctifying me, and for calling me to share your life forever.

No prophecy of scripture is a matter of one's own interpretation, because no prophecy ever came by human will, but men and women moved by the Holy Spirit spoke from God. 2 PETER 1:20–21

Who Has Spoken through the Prophets

ISAIAH 61:1–3 1*The spirit of the Lord God is upon me,*
because the Lord has anointed me;
he has sent me to bring good news to the oppressed,
to bind up the brokenhearted,
to proclaim liberty to the captives,
and release to the prisoners;
2*to proclaim the year of the Lord's favor,*
and the day of vengeance of our God;
to comfort all who mourn;
3*to provide for those who mourn in Zion—*
to give them a garland instead of ashes,
the oil of gladness instead of mourning,
the mantle of praise instead of a faint spirit.
They will be called oaks of righteousness,
the planting of the Lord, to display his glory.

1 PETER 1:10–12 10*Concerning this salvation, the prophets who prophesied of*
the grace that was to be yours made careful search and inquiry, 11*inquiring about*
the person or time that the Spirit of Christ within them indicated when it testified
in advance to the sufferings destined for Christ and the subsequent glory. 12*It was*

revealed to them that they were serving not themselves but you, in regard to the things that have now been announced to you through those who brought you good news by the Holy Spirit sent from heaven—things into which angels long to look!

2 PETER 1:19–21 [19]*So we have the prophetic message more fully confirmed. You will do well to be attentive to this as to a lamp shining in a dark place, until the day dawns and the morning star rises in your hearts.* [20]*First of all you must understand this, that no prophecy of scripture is a matter of one's own interpretation,* [21]*because no prophecy ever came by human will, but men and women moved by the Holy Spirit spoke from God.*

When we consider that the Holy Spirit "has spoken through the prophets," we think first of the prophets who spoke God's word throughout Israel's history. A prophet is one who is called and inspired by God to speak in God's name. Because "the Spirit of the Lord" descended upon the prophets of old, they spoke God's word to the people of Israel. We recall the prophets of Israel's historical books, like Nathan and Elijah, as well as the writing prophets, like Isaiah and Jeremiah. Yet, Moses, the source of Israel's Torah, is also considered a prophet, even greater than all the other prophets (Deut 34:10). So, the action of the Holy Spirit upon the prophets spans the entire Old Testament.

Jesus is the prophet God told Moses would come after him (Deut 18:18; Acts 7:37). Paul and the evangelists demonstrate how all the prophecies of Israel come to their completion in Jesus. The ideal prophetic figure who speaks in Isaiah's work, "The spirit of the Lord God is upon me, because the Lord has anointed me" (Isa 61:1), is ultimately Jesus himself. In Luke's gospel, Jesus reads this prophecy in the synagogue and then states, "Today this scripture has been fulfilled in your hearing" (Luke 4:18–21). In the life of Jesus, the word of God to Israel and the Spirit of God together produce an assurance of his own identity and ministry as God's Messiah. He is, par excellence, the one anointed by God's Spirit.

In declaring that the Holy Spirit "has spoken through the prophets," we profess the faith of Israel and of the church that God has truly revealed himself through the inspired words and actions of human beings. The prophets not only speak about God; they express God's word. Because the same Holy Spirit speaks through the history of Israel and into the life of Jesus and his church, the word of God in Scripture is fundamentally the same word in both the Old and the New Testaments. The revelation of God is a continuum through creation, Israel's history, the gospels, and the life of the church. The Holy Spirit has guided the entire saving plan throughout history, from old covenant to new covenant, from creation to new creation.

Peter's first letter demonstrates this great panorama of salvation by showing that it was the preexistent "Spirit of Christ" who inspired the ancient prophets to testify in advance to "the sufferings destined for Christ and the subsequent glory" (1 Pet 1:11). Those prophets of old were only able to glimpse this salvation from afar, but now Peter's Christian readers are able to experience the living Christ in his church. The salvation that the prophets foretold was taken up by early Christian missionaries who brought the "good news by the Holy Spirit sent from heaven" (1 Pet 1:12). Their preaching was inspired by the same divine Spirit who moved within the ancient prophets and now abides within the church.

Peter's second letter confirms that the prophetic message of the ancient Scriptures did not come from the prophets' own interpretation or the prophets' personal ideas. Rather, "men and women moved by the Holy Spirit spoke from God" (2 Pet 1:21). It is for this reason that their message must be carefully heeded, "like a lamp shining in a dark place" (2 Pet 1:19), a divine revelation illumining the ignorance of a darkened world. Therefore, readers of Scripture must look to the same Holy Spirit, the divine guidance alive within the church, to direct their understanding and application of the biblical texts. It is never enough to interpret Scripture by searching only for its historical meaning, as though it were merely a human composition. Instead, disciples of Jesus must be open to its "prophetic message," recognizing that God's inspired word speaks to every age and helps us discern the voice of God in the present.

Reflection and Discussion

- In what ways does the ministry of Jesus demonstrate that the prophetic words of Isaiah 61 have been fully completed in him?

- The Holy Spirit, poured out on the church at Pentecost, continues to raise up prophets in every age (Eph 4:11). How can Christians recognize prophets among us today? How might we discern the words and works of a genuine prophet?

- Why should I be as concerned to read the Old Testament as I am to read the New Testament? What can I do to better understand and reflect on the present meaning of Old Testament texts?

Prayer

Come, Holy Spirit, empower me to be an instrument of justice and healing in the places where I live and work. May my reading of Scripture enable me to stay faithful to the truth and guide me to discern prophetic voices in the world today.

SUGGESTIONS FOR FACILITATORS, GROUP SESSION 5

1. Welcome group members and ask if anyone has any questions, announcements, or requests.

2. You may want to pray this prayer as a group:
   Holy Spirit of the Living God, fall afresh on us and live within us, kindling in us the fire of divine love and guiding us to comprehend the mystery of salvation in all its richness. Live within our hearts to make us children of God, sharing in the divine nature and heirs of eternal life. Through our continuing reflection on Scripture, unbind us and transform us for a life of witness and service, empowering us to be instruments of justice and healing in the places where we live and work.

3. Ask one or both of the following questions:
   - What most intrigued you from this week's study?
   - How do the questions of Jesus help me to ask better questions of others?

4. Discuss lessons 19 through 24. Choose one or more of the questions for reflection and discussion from each lesson to talk over as a group.

5. Ask the group members to name one thing they have most appreciated about the way the group has worked during this Bible study. Ask group members to discuss any changes they might suggest in the way the group works in future studies.

6. Invite group members to complete lessons 25 through 30 on their own during the six days before the next meeting. They should write out their own answers to the questions as preparation for next week's session.

7. Discuss with group members ways in which studying the creed helps to make our weekly profession a genuine liturgical action.

8. Conclude by praying aloud together the prayer at the end of one of the lessons discussed. You may want to conclude the prayer by asking members to voice prayers of thanksgiving.

LESSON 25 SESSION 6

The gifts he gave were that some would be apostles, some prophets, some evangelists, some pastors and teachers, to equip the saints for the work of ministry, for building up the body of Christ.

EPHESIANS 4:11–12

One, Holy, Catholic, and Apostolic

EPHESIANS 2:19–22 *19 So then you are no longer strangers and aliens, but you are citizens with the saints and also members of the household of God, 20 built upon the foundation of the apostles and prophets, with Christ Jesus himself as the cornerstone. 21 In him the whole structure is joined together and grows into a holy temple in the Lord; 22 in whom you also are built together spiritually into a dwelling place for God.*

EPHESIANS 3:8–12 *8 Although I am the very least of all the saints, this grace was given to me to bring to the Gentiles the news of the boundless riches of Christ, 9 and to make everyone see what is the plan of the mystery hidden for ages in God who created all things; 10 so that through the church the wisdom of God in its rich variety might now be made known to the rulers and authorities in the heavenly places. 11 This was in accordance with the eternal purpose that he has carried out in Christ Jesus our Lord, 12 in whom we have access to God in boldness and confidence through faith in him.*

EPHESIANS 4:1–13 *1 I therefore, the prisoner in the Lord, beg you to lead a life worthy of the calling to which you have been called, 2 with all humility and gentleness, with patience, bearing with one another in love, 3 making every effort to main-*

tain the unity of the Spirit in the bond of peace. [4]There is one body and one Spirit, just as you were called to the one hope of your calling, [5]one Lord, one faith, one baptism, [6]one God and Father of all, who is above all and through all and in all.

[7]But each of us was given grace according to the measure of Christ's gift. [8]Therefore it is said,

> *"When he ascended on high he made captivity itself a captive;*
> *he gave gifts to his people."*

[9](When it says, "He ascended," what does it mean but that he had also descended into the lower parts of the earth? [10]He who descended is the same one who ascended far above all the heavens, so that he might fill all things.) [11]The gifts he gave were that some would be apostles, some prophets, some evangelists, some pastors and teachers, [12]to equip the saints for the work of ministry, for building up the body of Christ, [13]until all of us come to the unity of the faith and of the knowledge of the Son of God, to maturity, to the measure of the full stature of Christ.

The creed's article on the church depends entirely on the previous articles concerning belief in the Father, Son, and Holy Spirit. The origin of the church is in the divine Trinity, and the mission of the church is to be the sign and instrument of God's saving plan for the whole world. The Father called ancient Israel to be his own people and desired to gather all people as his own family. The Son inaugurated the church by proclaiming the gospel and forming a community of disciples who would continue his saving mission. And the Holy Spirit fills the church with wisdom and equips the church with manifold gifts of ministry to evangelize and teach all the nations. God desires that the church express divine love for all humanity and become the one People of God, the one Body of Christ, and the one Temple of the Holy Spirit.

Many people today desire to share in the life of Jesus Christ but not to associate themselves with his church. They claim that the Christian way has to do only with individual salvation and personal spirituality. This mindset is a striking break with the faith of early Christians and the testimony of the New Testament. The creed demonstrates that denying the necessity of the church is a distortion of authentic Christian faith, that excluding the church is a loss of something essential to the profession of faith. There are no

Christians in the New Testament except as members of Christ's church. The Scriptures always speak to this public assembly of believers who are together working out their salvation in Christ.

Of course, the Scriptures are well aware of the problems involved in God's choice to channel his saving grace through a frail, sinful, complex, institutional, messy human community. The prophets continually denounced the kings and priests of Israel for idolatry and injustice, and they show how the chastening of God's people was necessary for their return to the covenant. The church of the New Testament likewise distorted its witness to Christ by its corruption and dissension. The church has never been a faultless instrument of Christ's presence in the world. Yet, it is Christ's chosen instrument to witness to the gospel throughout the whole world. Filled with the Holy Spirit and promised the continual presence of the risen Christ until the end of the age, the community of disciples bears its exalted calling to be the church of Jesus Christ in the world.

The church exists in history but, at the same time, transcends it. The church is a visible reality, but at the same time a spiritual reality communicating divine life to the world. Yet, this earthly church equipped with hierarchical structures and the spiritual church endowed with heavenly riches are not to be thought of as two realities. Rather, they form one complex reality comprising a human and a divine element. With the eyes of faith, we can discern the divine, invisible, and timeless reality of the unique church of Christ, which we profess to be one, holy, catholic, and apostolic.

The unity of Christ's church is rooted in the oneness of God, the ultimate source of all unity. Paul describes the church as "one body" which is animated by "one Spirit" (Eph 4:4). This unified church strives toward its "one hope," the inheritance promised by the church's "one Lord" (4:5). The church is united in the "one faith," the gospel it professes, and "one baptism," through which each member is initiated into the life of Christ. This series of seven facets of the church's unity culminates in the origin of its unity, the "one God and Father of all" (4:6).

This one church has always been marked by great diversity. In fact, its unity in the Spirit allows and even requires a diversity of people and gifts. The one body, enlivened by the Spirit, is composed of diverse parts, all of which contribute to the body's unified functioning. When Christ ascended, the Spirit of Christ descended upon the church, making Christ accessible to all people everywhere at all times (4:7–10). This gift of God's grace is apportioned to each person in the form of spiritual gifts. In this way, all the parts of the body work together to produce the unified growth of the church. Some are "apostles" and "prophets," those witnesses and proclaimers who formed the church's foundation; some are "evangelists, some pastors and teachers," those who preach the gospel, shepherd the congregations, and feed the flock after the example of Jesus (4:11).

The church is holy because Christ is holy and he calls the church to be his bride, joining the church to himself as his body and endowing her with the gift of the Holy Spirit. In Christ and through his Spirit, the church "grows into a holy temple in the Lord," "a dwelling place for God" (2:21–22). The members of the church must always strive to express the church's essential holiness, to be witnesses to the presence of the risen Lord in the world.

The church is catholic because, by its very nature, it is both universal and inclusive of all. Paul argues that the church is essentially a place where the differences that divide people are reconciled. Paul's mission was "to bring to the Gentiles the news of the boundless riches of Christ" (3:8–9). He realized that the great wall of hostility that separated Jews and Gentiles is broken down in Christ and that God's mysterious plan to bring all people together in Christ is being accomplished through the church. All the polarities that divided people in Roman society—Jew and Gentile, slave and free person, woman and man, rich and poor—are reconciled in the catholic church. Every member of the church shares in the same task as Paul: to be sent out by Christ on a mission to the whole world.

Finally, the church is apostolic because it is "built upon the foundation of the apostles" (2:20), the witnesses chosen and sent on mission by Christ himself. The church is faithful to its apostolic origins as it hands on the teachings received from the apostles and as it continues the vocation of teaching, sanctifying, and guiding which Jesus gave to the apostles. The church continues the mission of Jesus in the world through the successors of the apostles until the end of time.

Reflection and Discussion

- In what ways do the Scriptures testify to the impossibility of fully living in Jesus Christ without sharing in his church? Why would God, despite all the risks involved, have chosen a human community in which to share divine life with the world?

- Because each of the four traditional marks of the church is both a gift of God's grace and a task for human effort and because the church must continually strive to embody these ideals, what are some specific ways that the church could better express itself as one, holy, catholic, and apostolic?

- Because Paul shows how the three great status markers of ancient society—ethnicity, class, and gender—are reconciled in Christ, how does the church continue to challenge our tendencies to divide people and associate only with people who are like-minded and similar to ourselves?

Prayer

Sovereign Lord, grant me the grace to lead a life worthy of the great calling you have given me. Make me your instrument in building up your church in the world and provide me with the spiritual gifts to put to the service of your church.

LESSON 26 SESSION 6

Rejoice in hope, be patient in suffering, persevere in prayer. Contribute to the needs of the saints; extend hospitality to strangers.

ROMANS 12:12–13

The Communion of Saints

ROMANS 12:1–18 [1]*I appeal to you therefore, brothers and sisters, by the mercies of God, to present your bodies as a living sacrifice, holy and acceptable to God, which is your spiritual worship.* [2]*Do not be conformed to this world, but be transformed by the renewing of your minds, so that you may discern what is the will of God—what is good and acceptable and perfect.*

[3]*For by the grace given to me I say to everyone among you not to think of yourself more highly than you ought to think, but to think with sober judgment, each according to the measure of faith that God has assigned.* [4]*For as in one body we have many members, and not all the members have the same function,* [5]*so we, who are many, are one body in Christ, and individually we are members one of another.* [6]*We have gifts that differ according to the grace given to us: prophecy, in proportion to faith;* [7]*ministry, in ministering; the teacher, in teaching;* [8]*the exhorter, in exhortation; the giver, in generosity; the leader, in diligence; the compassionate, in cheerfulness.*

[9]*Let love be genuine; hate what is evil, hold fast to what is good;* [10]*love one another with mutual affection; outdo one another in showing honor.* [11]*Do not lag in zeal, be ardent in spirit, serve the Lord.* [12]*Rejoice in hope, be patient in suffering, persevere in prayer.* [13]*Contribute to the needs of the saints; extend hospitality to strangers.*

[14]*Bless those who persecute you; bless and do not curse them.* [15]*Rejoice with those who rejoice, weep with those who weep.* [16]*Live in harmony with one another; do not be haughty, but associate with the lowly; do not claim to be wiser than you*

are. [17]*Do not repay anyone evil for evil, but take thought for what is noble in the*
sight of all. [18]*If it is possible, so far as it depends on you, live peaceably with all.*

HEBREWS 12:1–4 [1]*Therefore, since we are surrounded by so great a cloud of*
witnesses, let us also lay aside every weight and the sin that clings so closely, and
let us run with perseverance the race that is set before us, [2]*looking to Jesus the pio-*
neer and perfecter of our faith, who for the sake of the joy that was set before him
endured the cross, disregarding its shame, and has taken his seat at the right hand
of the throne of God.
[3]*Consider him who endured such hostility against himself from sinners, so that*
you may not grow weary or lose heart. [4]*In your struggle against sin you have not*
yet resisted to the point of shedding your blood.

The communion of saints is the intimate union that exists among all who are joined in faith and baptism to Jesus Christ. Some of his disciples are pilgrims on earth, others have died and are being purified, while others are in glory, contemplating God in full light. All who are in Christ and who share his Spirit are joined together to form one church. We form "one body in Christ, and individually we are members one of another" (Rom 12:5). Nothing, not even death, can separate Christians from Christ or from one another. Everyone joined in Christ participates in his life not only on earth but even more fully in the glory of heaven. This unity of believers invites us to pray and intercede for one another.

In a human family, members love one another and are concerned for the good of one another, turn to one another in times of joy and sorrow, and intercede for one another in times of trial and distress. Likewise, in the supernatural family of God, Christians love one another and are concerned with one another's growth and well-being, turning to one another for inspiration and intercession in times of need. The saints in heaven are intimately connected to us and care deeply about our lives on earth. They surround us like a "great cloud of witnesses" (Heb 12:1).

The communion of saints is most fully expressed in the celebration of the Eucharist. The church triumphant in heaven joins with the pilgrim church on earth to worship and offer thanksgiving to God. Joined with Jesus Christ and the eternal mystery of his saving death and resurrection, the whole church participates in the treasury of grace that he has given us. United with his sacrifice, we present our whole lives as an offering to God. Paul exhorts us: "Present your bodies as a living sacrifice, holy and acceptable to God, which is your spiritual worship" (Rom 12:1). When we unite our efforts with Christ's sacrifice, our daily prayers, works, joys, and sufferings are multiplied and given real power for the sanctification of ourselves and others.

If we have committed our lives to Christ, we are also committed to all his other disciples. Formed by Christ into his body, we belong to one another. Those who are strong in faith and rich in spiritual gifts have responsibilities to those who are weak in faith and lacking in grace. Those who are influential and wealthy have responsibilities to those who are poor and have no voice in society. This life of mutual commitment and belonging in the fellowship of the saints is full of practical consequences in the Christian life.

In addition to the saints in heaven, the word "saints" can refer to Christians on earth, who, whatever their personal sanctity as individuals, are called "holy ones" because they are consecrated to God and Christ. The letters of the New Testament are often addressed to the "saints" and refer to the work of these "saints" in the church. This does not mean that the church is a group of saintly people cloistered from the world. God calls us while we are sinners into a community within which his work of regeneration and renewal can take place. The church is a fellowship of forgiven sinners who confidently hope, by God's grace, to become a fellowship of saints.

Reflection and Discussion

- Because the communion of saints helps me envision the church as a great, universal family, with each member praying for and with the others, what can I do to heighten my awareness of the needs of Christians in other parts of the world?

- How do I understand the role of the saints in my own personal pilgrimage to heaven? On which saints do I particularly depend for support and intercession in my Christian life?

- Comparing the Christian life to running a race, while surrounded by a "cloud of witnesses" who have run the race before us, what advice does the author of Hebrews offer me for the challenges of Christian living?

- Remembering that I must use my strength to help those who may be weak and use my riches to help those who are poor, what can I do this week to express my solidarity with a struggling Christian?

Prayer

Lord God, may my love be genuine as I hold fast to what is good. Give me the zeal to contribute to the needs of the saints, extend hospitality to strangers, associate with the lowly, and live peaceably with all.

LESSON 27 SESSION 6

If we have died with Christ, we believe that we will also live with him. We know that Christ, being raised from the dead, will never die again; death no longer has dominion over him. ROMANS 6:8–9

I Confess One Baptism

ROMANS 6:3–11 *3 Do you not know that all of us who have been baptized into*
Christ Jesus were baptized into his death? 4 Therefore we have been buried with him
by baptism into death, so that, just as Christ was raised from the dead by the glory
of the Father, so we too might walk in newness of life.
5 For if we have been united with him in a death like his, we will certainly be
united with him in a resurrection like his. 6 We know that our old self was crucified
with him so that the body of sin might be destroyed, and we might no longer be
enslaved to sin. 7 For whoever has died is freed from sin. 8 But if we have died with
Christ, we believe that we will also live with him. 9 We know that Christ, being
raised from the dead, will never die again; death no longer has dominion over him.
10 The death he died, he died to sin, once for all; but the life he lives, he lives to God.
11 So you also must consider yourselves dead to sin and alive to God in Christ Jesus.

In Jesus' instructions at the end of Matthew's gospel, he exhorts his disciples to evangelize people of all nations, "baptizing them in the name of the Father and of the Son and of the Holy Spirit" (Matt 28:19). The letter to the Ephesians associates the church's "one baptism" with the unity of the church in "one Lord, one faith" (Eph 4:5). In his letter to the Romans, Paul explores the meaning and importance of baptism in the context of Christ's redemption.

The effect of baptism, Paul teaches, is a profound identification with Jesus, so that what is true of him becomes true of those who are baptized. When a person is "baptized into Christ Jesus," a very real change occurs: the believer dies with Christ and is born anew. The new Christian is transformed and intimately united with Christ and his Paschal Mystery.

Paul says that all of us who have been baptized were "baptized into his death" and even "buried with him" (verses 3–4). Since, by dying on the cross, Christ defeated sin, in our dying with Christ the power of sin no longer controls our lives. "Our old self was crucified" with Christ; therefore, the dominating influence of sin has been destroyed and we are no longer enslaved to it (verse 6).

But that is only half of our baptism. In dying, Christ conquered sin; in rising, he conquered death. As Christ was raised from the dead, we too have the vitality of eternal life within us, so "we too might walk in newness of life" (verse 4). While Paul describes our dying with Christ using verbs in the past tense, he describes our rising with Christ in the future tense: "We will certainly be united with him in a resurrection like his" and "we will also live with him" (verses 5, 8). The new life we have now is a prelude to our future resurrection. While we are truly "in Christ" by baptism, our lives are a step-by-step movement into Christlikeness.

The new creation that emerges from the waters of baptism has implications for the way we live each day. Paul insists that we no longer let sin reign in our bodies now that we have received the forgiveness that baptism gives: "So you also must consider yourselves dead to sin and alive to God in Christ Jesus" (verse 11). Since we are redeemed from sin and death, we must now live not as slaves but as children of God.

Baptism is an unrepeatable public initiation that expresses the embodied, incarnate reality of the Christian faith. Membership in Christ's body is not established through a private belief or an interior self-realization. Rather, baptism is a communal plunging of the initiate into the family of God, a joyful yet humbling experience. The ritual imprints the fundamental pattern of the Christian life on the believer: the saving mystery of Christ's dying and rising. It marks the believer as one belonging to the church, a redeemed community whose life demands a continual movement from slavery to freedom, acquisitiveness to generosity, darkness to light, fear to love, and death to life, modeled on and united with the living Lord and guided by the Holy Spirit.

Reflection and Discussion

- As the Christian initiation of new members of the church is the responsibility of all the baptized, what are some ways that I could support parents whose children are being baptized or encourage the catechumens of my parish preparing for baptism?

- Since baptism establishes a radical equality among all believers, offering all Christians a fundamental dignity as children of God and an equal responsibility for the body of Christ, how does confessing "one baptism" deepen my understanding of the church and my role in it?

- In making the sign of the cross, we remind ourselves that we are joined in baptism to the dying and rising of Jesus, in the name of the Father, and of the Son, and of the Holy Spirit. How can I be more fully aware of the baptismal meaning of the sign of the cross?

Prayer

Lord God, you have called me to be a new creation through my baptism into Christ Jesus. Since I have died with him, give me the grace to live through him and with him in the unity of the Holy Spirit. Help me to live as your child in the family of your church.

LESSON 28 **SESSION 6**

[Jesus] breathed on them and said to them, "Receive the Holy Spirit. If you forgive the sins of any, they are forgiven them; if you retain the sins of any, they are retained." JOHN 20:22–23

The Forgiveness of Sins

LUKE 15:18–24 [18]*"I will get up and go to my father, and I will say to him, 'Father,*
I have sinned against heaven and before you; [19]*I am no longer worthy to be called*
your son; treat me like one of your hired hands.' [20]*So he set off and went to his father.*
But while he was still far off, his father saw him and was filled with compassion;
he ran and put his arms around him and kissed him. [21]*Then the son said to him,*
'Father, I have sinned against heaven and before you; I am no longer worthy to be
called your son.' [22]*But the father said to his slaves, 'Quickly, bring out a robe—the*
best one—and put it on him; put a ring on his finger and sandals on his feet. [23]*And*
get the fatted calf and kill it, and let us eat and celebrate; [24]*for this son of mine was*
dead and is alive again; he was lost and is found!' And they began to celebrate.

JOHN 20:19–23 [19]*When it was evening on that day, the first day of the week, and*
the doors of the house where the disciples had met were locked for fear of the Jews,
Jesus came and stood among them and said, "Peace be with you." [20]*After he said*
this, he showed them his hands and his side. Then the disciples rejoiced when they
saw the Lord. [21]*Jesus said to them again, "Peace be with you. As the Father has sent*
me, so I send you." [22]*When he had said this, he breathed on them and said to them,*
"Receive the Holy Spirit. [23]*If you forgive the sins of any, they are forgiven them; if*
you retain the sins of any, they are retained."

2 CORINTHIANS 5:17–21 [17]*So if anyone is in Christ, there is a new creation: every-*
thing old has passed away; see, everything has become new! [18]*All this is from God,*

who reconciled us to himself through Christ, and has given us the ministry of reconciliation; [19]*that is, in Christ God was reconciling the world to himself, not counting their trespasses against them, and entrusting the message of reconciliation to us.* [20]*So we are ambassadors for Christ, since God is making his appeal through us; we entreat you on behalf of Christ, be reconciled to God.* [21]*For our sake he made him to be sin who knew no sin, so that in him we might become the righteousness of God.*

On the evening of the first Easter, Jesus appeared to his disciples and showed them the marks of his redeeming love in his hands and his side. He said to them, "As the Father has sent me, so I send you," commissioning them to carry on his saving ministry through his Spirit working within them. Then he breathed on them and said, "Receive the Holy Spirit. If you forgive the sins of any, they are forgiven them; if you retain the sins of any, they are retained" (John 20:21–23). In sharing with the church, through his apostles, the divine power to forgive sins, the risen Lord remits the sins of his people through the sacraments of his church.

The first and primary way in which sins are forgiven is the sacrament of baptism. Dying and rising with Christ in the sacramental waters, we are cleansed, forgiven, and walk in newness of life in the Holy Spirit. Yet, baptism does not deliver us from all the weakness of our nature. As baptized Christians in the early church fell into sin, the church began to discern how else it was called to forgive sins in the name of Christ. When Peter had asked how often he should forgive another member of the church, Jesus replied "seventy-seven times" (Matt 18:21–22). In other words, Jesus expressed the desire that in his church forgiveness should always be open to anyone who repents and turns away from sin.

The Apostles' Creed professes our belief in "the forgiveness of sins" immediately after its articles on "the holy catholic church" and "the communion of saints" because these mysteries of faith belong together. The forgiveness of sins is a ministry given to the church by the risen Lord. Jesus empowers his church to continue his own work of forgiveness of sins through the power of the Holy Spirit. As Jesus told the paralytic and the sinful woman, "Your sins are forgiven" (Matt 9:2; Luke 7:48), he empowers the church to continue to forgive in his name.

"The forgiveness of sins" was included in the Apostles' Creed at a time when those who had renounced their Christian faith during the persecutions were seeking mercy and restoration to the church. Throughout those early centuries, many who had committed grave sin after their baptism and sought forgiveness went through a public process of reconciliation through the church. The penitents did public penance for their sins and abstained from receiving the Eucharist. At the end of their time of penance, they were absolved of their sins and welcomed back into full communion with the church. Although rigorists criticized the pope and bishops for being too lenient in accepting grave sinners back to the church, the orthodox Catholic position permitted restoration after strict penance to assure true repentance.

Beneath the various forms which the sacrament of penance has taken over the centuries, its fundamental elements are twofold: first, the actions of those who turn back to God through the interior work of the Holy Spirit, and second, God's action in Christ through the mediation of his church. Penitents must express a genuine contrition for sin, thus opening their lives to God's healing grace. Penitents also make a verbal confession of sins, admitting the offense against God and the church. Then, God's action in Christ is mediated through the church's minister who prays the words of absolution over the repentant sinner.

Finally, penitents must do penance for the sin. The purpose of doing penance for sin is not to make up for sin or to merit forgiveness, which is offered only through the merits of the cross of Jesus. Its purpose, rather, is to express and strengthen our repentance. Penance usually takes the form of prayer, fasting, or almsgiving, expressing the penitent's active struggle against sin and cooperation with God's grace.

Through the church's "ministry of reconciliation," the repentant sinner is forgiven by God and reconciled to the church (2 Cor 5:18). Paul's letter highlights the fact that sin is not just a private matter between the sinner and God. Rather, the sins of one member of the community affect the whole church. Likewise, forgiveness is not just a private, spiritual concern but a communal affair. Reconciliation with the church is inseparable from reconciliation with God. The church's ministry of reconciliation is the task of making known God's reconciling activity in Christ and serving as an instrument of that grace in the world.

Knowing the depths of the Father's love, Jesus reveals his tender mercy in the profoundly genuine story of the prodigal son. The parable contains all the elements of the sacramental process of reconciliation: sin, repentance, confession, forgiveness, and restoration to the family table. Regretting his sin, the son admits his foolishness and the wrong he has committed, not only against himself but against the well-being of his whole family. Turning around, he begins to walk back home, resolved to declare his guilt before his father. This first move is sufficient for the father to begin pouring out his mercy. Spotting his son a long way off, the father runs to his son and embraces him with tender compassion. As the son confesses his sins, the father is bent on helping him reverse his shame and welcomes him to the family feast. The story is that of a lost child and the journey of return to his father's house and family, the church.

Reflection and Discussion

- Considering the church's early history, why do grave sins require a sacramental process of reconciliation through the church?

- Why might praying, fasting, and almsgiving as penance for sin help me to avoid sin in the future?

- As Jesus' parable of the prodigal son shows the relationship between repentance, confession, and forgiveness, how does the parable help me to understand more personally each of these three elements of the church's ministry of reconciliation?

Prayer

Father of mercy, through the death and resurrection of your Son, you have reconciled the world to yourself, and you have sent the Holy Spirit for the forgiveness of sins. I pray for a spirit of repentance for my sins and for the peace that comes from your healing love.

LESSON 29 SESSION 6

What is sown is perishable, what is raised is imperishable. It is sown in dishonor, it is raised in glory. It is sown in weakness, it is raised in power. It is sown a physical body, it is raised a spiritual body.

1 CORINTHIANS 15:42–44

I Look Forward to the Resurrection of the Dead

1 CORINTHIANS 15:35–58 [35]*But someone will ask, "How are the dead raised? With what kind of body do they come?"* [36]*Fool! What you sow does not come to life unless it dies.* [37]*And as for what you sow, you do not sow the body that is to be, but a bare seed, perhaps of wheat or of some other grain.* [38]*But God gives it a body as he has chosen, and to each kind of seed its own body.* [39]*Not all flesh is alike, but there is one flesh for human beings, another for animals, another for birds, and another for fish.* [40]*There are both heavenly bodies and earthly bodies, but the glory of the heavenly is one thing, and that of the earthly is another.* [41]*There is one glory of the sun, and another glory of the moon, and another glory of the stars; indeed, star differs from star in glory.*

[42]*So it is with the resurrection of the dead. What is sown is perishable, what is raised is imperishable.* [43]*It is sown in dishonor, it is raised in glory. It is sown in weakness, it is raised in power.* [44]*It is sown a physical body, it is raised a spiritual body. If there is a physical body, there is also a spiritual body.* [45]*Thus it is written, "The first man, Adam, became a living being"; the last Adam became a life-giving spirit.* [46]*But it is not the spiritual that is first, but the physical, and then the spiritual.* [47]*The first man was from the earth, a man of dust; the second man is from heaven.* [48]*As was the man of dust, so are those who are of the dust; and as is the*

man of heaven, so are those who are of heaven. 49 *Just as we have borne the image of the man of dust, we will also bear the image of the man of heaven.*

50 *What I am saying, brothers and sisters, is this: flesh and blood cannot inherit the kingdom of God, nor does the perishable inherit the imperishable.* 51 *Listen,*
I will tell you a mystery! We will not all die, but we will all be changed, 52 *in a*
moment, in the twinkling of an eye, at the last trumpet. For the trumpet will sound,
and the dead will be raised imperishable, and we will be changed. 53 *For this perish-*
able body must put on imperishability, and this mortal body must put on immor-
tality. 54 *When this perishable body puts on imperishability, and this mortal body*
puts on immortality, then the saying that is written will be fulfilled:

"Death has been swallowed up in victory."
55 *"Where, O death, is your victory?*
Where, O death, is your sting?"

56 *The sting of death is sin, and the power of sin is the law.* 57 *But thanks be to God,*
who gives us the victory through our Lord Jesus Christ.

58 *Therefore, my beloved, be steadfast, immovable, always excelling in the work of the Lord, because you know that in the Lord your labor is not in vain.*

The concluding phrases of the creed offer us a compelling call to live an optimistic life, full of hope in God. The resurrection of the body that we await is firmly planted in the resurrection of Jesus Christ himself. We can't escape death, but we can overcome it in Christ. Although our physical frames wear out with age and waste away toward their inevitable end, we are not daunted in the face of death because we trust in God's promises of resurrection.

Because resurrection is far beyond anything we have ever experienced or anything we can fully comprehend, we ask questions much like those addressed to Paul: "How are the dead raised? With what kind of body do they come?" (verse 35). The Corinthians naively assumed that resurrection of the dead referred to the resuscitation of corpses. Paul explains that resurrection entails transformation of the body into a new and glorious state. Because human language is incapable of adequately expressing the reality of resurrection, Paul turns to metaphors and analogies to help his hearers understand.

Paul first uses the image of a plant springing forth from a seed (verses 36–38). The seed sown in the ground first dies, then it grows into a mature plant. No one could predict the form of the plant from the appearance of the seed. God is the one who determines what sort of body to give it. With this analogy, Paul is able to demonstrate both the radical transformation of the human body in its resurrected state and yet its organic continuity with the mortal body that preceded it. Since our glorified state is indeed an embodied existence, Paul demonstrates that there are many different kinds of bodies in God's creation (verses 39–41). Each has its own distinct form, from the variety of animal life to the diverse heavenly bodies in the sky. Since each of these bodies possess varying degrees of glory, we can more easily imagine a different kind of human body, a glorified body unlike the bodies we now know.

Resurrection involves transformation into a new kind of body suitable for its new form of existence (verses 42–44). The body in this present life is perishable and weak; the body of those resurrected from the dead will be imperishable and glorious. What is sown is a natural, physical body; what is raised is a supernatural, spiritual body. Paul uses the representational figures of Adam and Christ to contrast humanity in its natural life and in its spiritual life to come (verses 45–49). We inherit one kind of body and life from Adam, "the man of dust," followed by a renewed, transformed body from Christ, "the man of heaven." We await the day when Christ, manifested in his resurrected body, will come from heaven to raise us and transform us into his likeness. On that final day, "we will all be changed" (verses 51–52), both the dead and those still alive, and our perishable, mortal bodies will put on imperishability and immortality (verses 53–54).

Although the "how" of resurrection remains a mystery, we know that God's plan for the end is not to destroy our bodies and start again but to transform our bodies, not to reject his creation but to redeem it. God's ultimate victory over death is already assured, so we can even today sing a taunting victory song over the fallen enemy: "Where, O death, is your victory? Where, O death, is your sting?" (verses 55, 57). Death's stinging power to evoke fear, depression, and despair is already defeated through our Lord Jesus Christ.

The final consequence of Christ's victory over death is stated in the last verse: We can do the work of the Lord with confident faith, knowing that in him everything we do has ultimate meaning and purpose (verse 58). Nothing we do in Christ is ever "in vain." We face life with an eternal perspective. We may not see the harvest of our work in our own lifetime, but a harvest there will indeed be.

Reflection and Discussion

- Christians do not hope in just survival after death, the consequence of having an immortal soul or the continual repetition of mortal life through reincarnation. In what sense is Christian salvation far richer than simply ongoing life after death?

- Because Christian hope is confident and assured, relying on God's faithfulness and constancy, how has this hope sustained me in times of suffering and trial?

- What motivates the work that I do? Remembering Paul's encouragement, "You know that in the Lord your labor is not in vain," how does he inspire me to work with steadfastness and hope?

Prayer

Thanks be to God who gives us the victory through our Lord Jesus Christ. You have destroyed the powers of death and given us hope and confidence in the future. Help me to live a life that is worth living for eternity.

LESSON 30 SESSION 6

They will see his face, and his name will be on their foreheads. And there will be no more night; they need no light of lamp or sun, for the Lord God will be their light, and they will reign forever and ever.

REVELATION 22:4–5

And the Life of the World to Come

JOHN 11:21–27 21 *Martha said to Jesus, "Lord, if you had been here, my brother*
would not have died. 22 *But even now I know that God will give you whatever you*
ask of him." 23 *Jesus said to her, "Your brother will rise again."* 24 *Martha said to*
him, "I know that he will rise again in the resurrection on the last day." 25 *Jesus said*
to her, "I am the resurrection and the life. Those who believe in me, even though
they die, will live, 26 *and everyone who lives and believes in me will never die. Do*
you believe this?" 27 *She said to him, "Yes, Lord, I believe that you are the Messiah,*
the Son of God, the one coming into the world."

REVELATION 22 1 *Then the angel showed me the river of the water of life, bright as*
crystal, flowing from the throne of God and of the Lamb 2 *through the middle of the*
street of the city. On either side of the river is the tree of life with its twelve kinds of
fruit, producing its fruit each month; and the leaves of the tree are for the healing
of the nations. 3 *Nothing accursed will be found there any more. But the throne of*
God and of the Lamb will be in it, and his servants will worship him; 4 *they will see*
his face, and his name will be on their foreheads. 5 *And there will be no more night;*
they need no light of lamp or sun, for the Lord God will be their light, and they will
reign forever and ever.

6And he said to me, "These words are trustworthy and true, for the Lord, the God of the spirits of the prophets, has sent his angel to show his servants what must soon take place."

7"See, I am coming soon! Blessed is the one who keeps the words of the prophecy of this book."

8I, John, am the one who heard and saw these things. And when I heard and saw them, I fell down to worship at the feet of the angel who showed them to me; 9but he said to me, "You must not do that! I am a fellow servant with you and your comrades the prophets, and with those who keep the words of this book. Worship God!"

10And he said to me, "Do not seal up the words of the prophecy of this book, for the time is near. 11Let the evildoer still do evil, and the filthy still be filthy, and the righteous still do right, and the holy still be holy."

12"See, I am coming soon; my reward is with me, to repay according to everyone's work. 13I am the Alpha and the Omega, the first and the last, the beginning and the end."

14Blessed are those who wash their robes, so that they will have the right to the tree of life and may enter the city by the gates. 15Outside are the dogs and sorcerers and fornicators and murderers and idolaters, and everyone who loves and practices falsehood.

16"It is I, Jesus, who sent my angel to you with this testimony for the churches. I am the root and the descendant of David, the bright morning star."

17The Spirit and the bride say, "Come."
And let everyone who hears say, "Come."
And let everyone who is thirsty come.
Let anyone who wishes take the water of life as a gift.

18I warn everyone who hears the words of the prophecy of this book: if anyone adds to them, God will add to that person the plagues described in this book; 19if anyone takes away from the words of the book of this prophecy, God will take away that person's share in the tree of life and in the holy city, which are described in this book.

20The one who testifies to these things says, "Surely I am coming soon." Amen. Come, Lord Jesus!

21The grace of the Lord Jesus be with all the saints. Amen.

Concerning the future, the creed affirms that Jesus Christ will come again in glory to judge the living and the dead, and his kingdom will have no end. For this reason, we look forward to the resurrection of the dead and the life of the world to come. These truths animate the Christian worldview, bringing eternal purpose to our present lives.

The theme of life dominates the Gospel of John, from beginning to end. Jesus states that his purpose in coming is to share life everlasting: "I came that they may have life, and have it abundantly" (10:10; 20:31). Throughout the gospel, Jesus demonstrates this purpose through a series of signs which culminate in his confrontation with death at the raising of Lazarus. Jesus says, "I am the resurrection and the life" (11:25). First, Jesus is our resurrection: "Those who believe in me, even though they die, will live." For those united with Jesus through faith, death will not cut them off from the life God gives, and God will raise them up on the last day. Second, Jesus is our life: "Everyone who lives and believes in me will never die." The eternal life that we begin to experience now through faith in Jesus will never be extinguished, not even by death. Union with Jesus brings us eternal life in the present; resurrection on the last day will bring that life to its fullness. Resurrection and eternal life are the fruit of a relationship with Jesus. Where Jesus is, there is life that never ends and the hope of resurrection. This blessed communion of life with all who are perfectly united with Christ, the fulfillment of the deepest human longings, is called heaven. This state of supreme happiness is beyond all earthly understanding and can only be expressed with metaphorical images in Scripture. St. Cyprian, the third-century bishop of Carthage, wrote of those seeing God in heaven: "How great will your glory and happiness be, to be allowed to see God, to be honored with sharing the joy of salvation and eternal light with Christ your Lord and God…to delight in the joy of immortality in the Kingdom of heaven with the righteous and God's friends" (Cyprian, *Ep.* 58, 10,1: CSEL 3/2, 665).

The last chapter of the Bible offers a fitting reflection on the last article of the creed. After all the sound and fury of the book of Revelation, God has the last word, and it is a word of life. The final vision that the angel shows to John symbolizes the new creation, the complete fulfillment of God's plan for the world's salvation. It is Paradise restored, with a river flowing through the streets of the new Jerusalem and the tree of life producing fruit for all. In the midst of this perfected creation stands the throne of God and the Lamb. There we will worship God and see his face, and God's name will be on our foreheads, signifying how precious we are to him.

Throughout the book of Revelation, John has sought to fill us with confidence in Christ's ultimate victory, so that we will choose to follow him wherever he leads us. This final vision teaches us that the fullness of life that awaits us fulfills all the hopes of Scripture. Beyond all the tears and pain of humanity's history, men and women find life with God and "they will reign forever and ever" (verse 5). After many images of God's righteous anger and fierce justice, we are left with a final picture of God's unimaginable mercy and love.

Jesus is the Alpha and the Omega, from creation to new creation, the beginning and the end of all human desire (verse 13). He is the "bright morning star" whose rising begins the never-ending day of eternity (verse 16). The ancient liturgical prayer of the church, "Come, Lord Jesus!" the final prayer of the Bible, must be just as urgent and heartfelt for us as it was for the early Christians. The imminence of his return is not just a matter of chronological time. We are called by God's inspired word to live as if Jesus were returning today, as if we were to give an account of our lives to God in the next hour. God's kingdom has already drawn near to us, and God wants us to live in anticipation of its full arrival.

Both the last book of the Bible and the creed end with the word "Amen." The root of this Hebrew word expresses confidence, faithfulness, and trustworthiness, the same root as the word translated "believe." To believe is to say "Amen" to God's words, promises, and saving plan. Thus, the creed's final "Amen" confirms its first words, "I believe." It indicates our confident acceptance of what we have just professed.

Reflection and Discussion

- How would my life be different if I knew that Christ was coming in glory tomorrow? What is preventing me from living that way today?

- What does it mean to address Jesus as the Alpha and Omega? In light of the biblical testimony and the formulations of the creed, how is he the first and the last, the beginning and the end?

- Professing the creed is not only making a personal statement but a liturgical act. Considering the full meaning of Christian faith and belief, what does it mean to say "Amen" to the words of the creed?

- What are some of the primary insights I recall from this study? What do I wish to remember when I recite the creed during the Mass this week?

Prayer

Come, Lord Jesus, come and fill your creation with your glorious presence. Fill me with your life and give me the grace to live each day in anticipation of your glorious coming.

SUGGESTIONS FOR FACILITATORS, GROUP SESSION 6

1. Welcome group members and make any final announcements or requests.

2. You may want to pray this prayer as a group:
   Lord Jesus Christ, you have formed your church on the faith of the apostles and commissioned it to evangelize, baptize, and teach your word to a waiting world. Make us your instruments in building up your church and provide us with spiritual gifts to put to the service of your church. May we contribute to the needs of the saints, extend welcome to strangers, associate with the lowly, and lead lives worthy of the great calling you have given us. Give us the grace to live each day in anticipation of your glorious coming.

3. Ask one or both of the following questions:
   - How has this study of the creed deepened your life in Christ?
   - In what way has this study challenged you the most?

4. Discuss lessons 25 through 30. Choose one or more of the questions for reflection and discussion from each lesson to discuss as a group.

5. Ask the group if they would like to study another book in the *Threshold Bible Study* series. Discuss the topic and dates, and make a decision among those interested. Ask the group members to suggest people they would like to invite to participate in the next study series.

6. Ask the group to discuss the insights that stand out most from this study over the past six weeks.

7. Conclude by praying aloud the following prayer or another of your own choosing:
   Holy Spirit of the living God, you inspired the writers of the Scriptures, and you have guided our study during these weeks. Continue to deepen our love for the word of God in the holy Scriptures, and draw us more deeply into the heart of Jesus. Thank you for your merciful, gracious, steadfast, and faithful love.